Girl Dad Energy Unleashed

What Baby Girl Needs From You:
A New Dad Survival Guide To Bond,
Support and Thrive In Her First Year

Tyler Upfield

© Copyright 2025 - All rights reserved.

The content contained within this book may not be reproduced, duplicated or transmitted without direct written permission from the author or the publisher.

Under no circumstances will any blame or legal responsibility be held against the publisher, or author, for any damages, reparation, or monetary loss due to the information contained within this book, either directly or indirectly.

Legal Notice:

This book is copyright protected. It is only for personal use. You cannot amend, distribute, sell, use, quote or paraphrase any part, or the content within this book, without the consent of the author or publisher.

Disclaimer Notice:

Please note the information contained within this document is for educational and entertainment purposes only. All effort has been executed to present accurate, up to date, reliable, complete information. No warranties of any kind are declared or implied. Readers acknowledge that the author is not engaged in the rendering of legal, financial, medical or professional advice. The content within this book has been derived from various sources. Please consult a licensed professional before attempting any techniques outlined in this book.

By reading this document, the reader agrees that under no circumstances is the author responsible for any losses, direct or indirect, that are incurred as a result of the use of the information contained within this document, including, but not limited to, errors, omissions, or inaccuracies.

Table of Contents

INTRODUCTION 1

CHAPTER 1: WHAT JUST HAPPENED? 5
    WE'RE PREGNANT! 5
    THE WAITING ROOM OF PREGNANCY 6
    READY OR NOT, HERE SHE COMES! 10
    THE AWKWARD MIRACLE OF LIFE 11
    THE BIRTH ESSENTIALS KIT 13

CHAPTER 2: YOU'RE IN IT NOW! 15
    ADAPT OR DIE 15
    FINDING WHAT'S IMPORTANT 16
    ROLE CONFUSION 18
    FEELING KINDA BLUE 19
    LOOKING AFTER NUMBER ONE 21
    THE GIRL DAD ROLE KIT 22

CHAPTER 3: GETTING STUCK IN 23
    UNFAMILIAR TERRITORY 24
    THE UPSIDE OF HANDS-ON 25
    DADS ON BOARD 26
    GOOD CONNECTIONS 27
    THE LONG GAME 30
    THE BONDING KIT 32

CHAPTER 4: "EXTRA"-ORDINARY DADS 33
    FILLING THE ROLE 34
    NO MISTAKE, NO REGRET 35
    THE GIRL DAD STEP-UP KIT 36

CHAPTER 5: BECOMING DADDY 37
    FATHERS AND DADS 38
    FEED, CHANGE, REPEAT 39
        Search for Clues 39
        Following Patterns 40
    DADDY'S LITTLE GIRL 41

WHAT'S THE DIFFERENCE?	43
WATCHING AND LEARNING	44
THE OUT-OF-THE-HOUSE SURVIVAL KIT	46

CHAPTER 6: SCREWING UP (AGAIN!) 47

PRESSURE TO PERFORM	48
WORST FEARS	49
LOSING IT	52
DEALING WITH MISTAKES	53
LESSONS FOR LIFE	54
THE RESILIENCE KIT	56

CHAPTER 7: THREE'S A CROWD 57

OUT OF BALANCE	58
ON THE SAME TEAM	59
REIGNITING THE SPARK	61
BETWEEN THE SHEETS	63
THE RELATIONSHIP RESET KIT	66

CHAPTER 8: SURVIVAL OF THE FITTEST 67

MILKING EVERY MOMENT	67
BECOMING A LITTLE PERSON	69
SELF-PRESERVATION	71
Physical	*71*
Mental	*72*
Social	*73*
I GET BY WITH A LITTLE HELP	74
INSIDER INFO	75
THE FIRST-YEAR RHYTHM KIT	77

CHAPTER 9: CHOOSING FOR TOMORROW 79

FAMILY FIRST	80
A MORAL GUIDE	82
Passions	*83*
Values	*83*
Beliefs	*84*
Strengths and Weaknesses	*84*
DIFFICULT DILEMMAS	85
No Clear-Cut Choice	*86*
Facing the Backlash	*86*
LEAVING A LEGACY	87
THE LONG-TERM GIRL DAD KIT	89

CONCLUSION 91

THE REMEMBER-AND-LAUGH KIT 93
REFERENCES **96**

Introduction

I don't know *everything* about being a dad!

That's probably not what you want to hear as you're about to read a book on becoming a new father… but it's the truth!

My credentials? No degree in paediatrics, very little experience in parenting, no idea about child psychology, and zero social media clout… Really, I'm not a dad-guru; I'm just a typical Millennial. Someone who lived with his parents until he was 24, and who had never booked his own doctor's appointments. A gamer, party animal, and live-life-as-it-comes type of dude. For me, there was no real need to grow up, no pressure to do or become.

That is… until the day I held my little baby girl in my arms. I had to step up and learn quickly, like a small bird pushed out of the nest, flapping, flailing, falling, and hoping not to hit the ground.

This book is about all that—the honesty of someone finding his way on the fly. And while the pages are a bit thin on all the clinical statistics and psychology quotes, they are teeming with brutal, true-to-life stories and tips. In this day and age, where every Google fact needs to be double-checked to know if it's a fake or not, the open, exposed, vulnerable truth of someone's experiences speaks much louder.

That's where I come in!

These chapters are filled with my insecurities:

- *Will I be a good enough dad?*
- *Will this little girl ever love me?*

- *Will I be like my own dad?*
- *What about my wife? Will our relationship survive?*

You'll also discover my fears:

- Passing out in the delivery room.
- Puking while changing diapers.
- Falling asleep at work.
- Dropping my daughter on her head.

And I'll even let you in on my joys:

- Falling in love… *again*!
- Seeing that first smile.
- Becoming a family.

Look, this is not a parental guide. It's not a DIY book. And it's certainly not a lecture. It's raw, honest life.

But, before you think this is just an autobiography of a sleep-deprived first-time dad, don't despair. There are plenty of helpful tools and tricks (and a few stats) I've picked up along the way. Because even though this is my journey, it's not all about me! This is so much bigger. This book is about every normal guy out there, like yourself, struggling to figure out how to become a father. It's for every single man who has been thrown into the deep end of fatherhood. In short, it's about you and me.

As I sifted through what really matters and what doesn't, I really aimed to lay it all out for you in the most helpful way. Why? Because I want you to step up and build a bond with your kid that will last for the rest of your life. The mess-ups and the victories are not just me bearing myself. They are in here for you to identify with, learn from, and adapt for your own life.

My guess is that if you're reading this, you're already in a tailspin, or you're about to get pushed out of the tree. You might feel completely unprepared, as I was. But you're willing to grow, and that's all that counts. The fact that you want to be the best you possibly can be is enough of a place to start. That's exactly where I was…

On that note, here's a little mantra for you: *Your presence matters way more than your perfection!*

In the coming pages, I've included some great little tips that can really end up being game-changers, helping you progress to the next level. If you're a gamer like me, then you'll appreciate the tag of cheat code for each one. They're like easter eggs, loopholes, and shortcuts that are handy to have in your back pocket! And if that's not enough, you'll find links to cheat sheets and other helpful downloadable files at the end of each chapter in the form of easy-to-use girl dad kits.

I still don't know everything… and I probably never will! Each situation is unique, and there is always so much to learn. So, you're in good company if you don't want to compare yourself with all the other "super-dads" who are doing their best to keep it together.

With all that said, then, walk with me as I journey through the first roller-coaster year of having a daughter. Grab hold as we fall headfirst into that scary world of becoming a dad. Don't worry… if I survived it, you can too!

Tyler

Chapter 1:

What Just Happened?

The guys who fear becoming fathers don't understand that fathering is not something perfect men do, but something that perfects the man.
—Frank Pittman

Joy and fear.

Two highly impulsive emotions. One propels you up through the clouds so fast, your head is spinning with elation. The other drags you deep into a dark corner where you can't breathe. These are two reactive, combustible chemicals that are tough to contain on their own, so, I'll go out on a limb and say it's best if they're kept separate. They simply shouldn't mix.

And yet, I felt both... at the same time! My chest wanted to *explode*!

It was kinda like sitting in the roller coaster car at the very top, staring at that rail falling away beneath you. Exhilaration and absolute terror combined. *Should I stay or should I go?* Or talking to your crush for the very first time at school... sweaty palms, trembling knees, dry mouth— you just want to die, and yet there's a heavenly awe you're caught up in because, well, she actually noticed you! And what about showing up for work on the first day, feeling super proud of yourself, but totally out of your depth? There are so many pivotal moments where you want to go forward but are afraid of falling off the edge!

We're Pregnant!

And there I was... Tyler, completely in over my head when my partner said she was pregnant. I wanted to dance, hug her, and shout it out for everyone to hear. But I also wanted to hit pause (or even rewind) and scream my lungs out! I needed proof, first off, and asked to see the pregnancy test. It wasn't because I didn't believe her or anything, I just needed some convincing because I was nowhere near being ready.

It was a gut-punch, simply put. My world was about to flip on its side, and I would no longer be the one in control. It wasn't a total surprise, of course, as we had spoken about having a baby and had done some planning for it. It was more of a shock, then, to realize we were *actually* going to be parents! At the time, I was still texting my mom and dad for advice on how to fix a burnt dinner. *How was I supposed to make decisions for someone else?*

In a study (Smith & McDonald, 2022), a group of guys who reluctantly or unexpectedly became fathers admitted feeling "regret, sadness, guilt… or like the tin man without a heart," while others were "happy but freaking out and simultaneously scared, hopeful, excited, terrified." Truly, a whirlwind of emotions is a very normal reaction.

It wasn't the last time I would have that nauseating grip of terror mixed with pure elation. I was about to learn that becoming a dad was a lifelong series of ups and downs, each with its unique joys and distinct moments of panic. Strapping into that roller coaster car seat of fatherhood, as it clacked its way up the steep track, was going to be terrifically scary, but at the same time, the most ultimately rewarding ride of my life!

The Waiting Room of Pregnancy

The next time joy and fear turned up together and pummeled me like a tsunami was in the delivery room. But I'm getting ahead of myself… nine months ahead, in fact!

If the baby being born is the tipping point of the roller coaster, where it all starts happening, then the pregnancy is the slow incline. That clickety-clack as the car makes its way painstakingly up to the top… There's no other way to get there but to endure it. At first, I was so excited that Renee was pregnant, but after the first month, I was over it! The romantic movie montage screeched to a halt as I held her hair back so she could vomit yet again. I just wanted to be a dad and play games with my kid, but this was definitely something else.

I felt like I was a spectator, another number in the bank queue, waiting for something to happen. Guys can easily feel sidelined and helpless, even signing off during the months leading up to the big day. It's normal to suddenly feel like a backup parent, a substitute waiting to get into the game.

I learned the hard way that my role was just as important as hers was. Sure, she was carrying our kid, doing all the hard work, but instead of tuning out, I could also *be there*. After complaining that I hadn't slept well, I realized things were different. Renee's body was changing drastically; she was constantly going to pee, and felt bloated and ugly. Needless to say, I spent a night on the couch!

It dawned on me that night: *If I wanted to be a father to my baby girl, it would begin with taking care of the person carrying her.* After all, I was half responsible for all of this! While Renee seemed to have it under control, she desperately needed my assurance. My being there was more important than if I knew all the medical terms for the trimesters! She needed me to be an anchor, even though I felt as though I was freewheeling off a cliff face.

So, instead of whipping on a red cape and trying to save the world, I took it step by step, day by day. I learned as I went along and found it easier to break the pregnancy period up into three bite-sized roles.

- **Helper:**
    - In the first three months, Renee went through a wild swing of emotions, from throwing up to craving mozzarella sticks at 2 a.m. to being generally wiped out by the evening. It was not easy predicting her behavior as she didn't even know what she was feeling or wanted. All I could do was be there in any way possible.

- Step up by cooking when she can't (stay away from foods that make her nauseous!).
- Show an interest by accompanying her to the doctor or attending prenatal classes.
- Go out and get medicine or snacks, no matter what time it is!

- **Pamperer:**
  - During the next three-month phase, things calmed down a bit during this phase, and Renee was much more relaxed, bouncy, and glowing. They call it the honeymoon period! So, I focused on spoiling her.
  - Lotions, bath salts, and gifts are always a winner.
  - A weekend away might be the perfect answer to reintroducing some romance!
  - Massages. That goes without saying.

- **Comforter:**
  - Renee wasn't the happiest toward the end of the nine months. The discomfort, extra weight, and effort to get things done began to take their toll. I had to learn to make everything as easy as possible as we both got ready for D-Day!
  - Let her put her feet up whenever she needs, while you do the cooking or cleaning.
  - If you go out, make sure it's easy for her to get to the bathroom quickly.
  - Build up her self-esteem—beautiful and radiant are good answers when she asks if she looks fat!

- Don't be grumpy if she keeps you awake—expectant mothers suffer from insomnia.

Now, you may read this and think that I was the perfect partner throughout the pregnancy, doing everything I could for the love of my life and my soon-to-be-born daughter. But I missed the mark on numerous occasions: I opened my dumb mouth too often without thinking, I didn't really understand what she was going through all the time, and sometimes I just tapped out. I know, it sounds selfish, but it happens. The key is getting back in the game and being there despite the failures.

- **Cheat Code:** Shut up!

    Too many guys have messed up by being harsh, selfish, or too honest. *Think it, but don't say it.* This will help smooth over some moments that turn awkward and lead to really big problems later on. If you want to survive as a couple, stay away from these lines: "Do I have to be here?", "This is taking forever," "I know how you feel," or "Why are you crying again?"

The good news is you're not alone. Hundreds and thousands of men are grappling with the shockwave of joy and fear. Realizing I was not alone absolutely helped, and talking it through allowed me to see that what I was going through and feeling was normal.

Ross, a dad-to-be, had this to say: "It's so reassuring to talk to other parents-to-be who are experiencing a similar rollercoaster of events" (Tommy's, 2022).

A.J., another new proud father, put it like this:

> It's important that the mum gets all the support she needs, but I think men need a support network too. I'm lucky to have close friends who are dads and we've been friends for a long time so that support is already there. But I can imagine that a man who doesn't have that network could feel lonely (Tommy's, 2022, para. 8).

Ready or Not, Here She Comes!

Those nine months seemed to drag at times, and I often had to remind myself that I was a part of this whole journey. And then suddenly, boom—we were at the hospital. Funny how something you are so prepared for can catch you with your pants down! The overnight bag was prepped, frozen meals were in the freezer, and everyone was on standby. And yet when Renee's water broke, I felt like a headless chicken. Once again, I was ambushed by the lethal combo of joy and fear.

Some dads think that because it's a C-section (where the baby is delivered by surgical incision), there's no worry or real reason to get too involved. They see it as a shortcut, but it's not. A birth is a birth, no matter which way it happens. Both mom and daughter need you as much as if it were a 12-hour labor! There will still be pain, anxiety, and exhaustion.

As a Millennial, I Googled everything about giving birth. I mean, it's better to know what you're getting yourself into than being sideswiped on the day. I'm not lying, but there are some rather graphic explanations if you can handle them. For me, one that really helped was a simple video on YouTube by Liz Chalmers using a ping-pong ball and a balloon (Miller, 2017). After that, I truly had so much respect for Renee!

Here's an important thing to note: No two births are exactly alike. Whether it's hypnobirthing, a water birth, or a surgical procedure, each one is unique. Indeed, what you see in the movies might be vastly different from what you and your partner experience. Renee underwent a C-section in the end. It just happened to be the best choice for us as a family at the time.

There I was in my ill-fitting hospital scrubs, a mask hiding my grimace of panic. No soft glow for the ambience, no background tunes filtering through the hospital sound system, and definitely no calm one-liners as doctors worked to ensure our little girl arrived safely. Sterile lights and the pervading smell of antiseptic were our only companions. But none of that was important... This was no film set, no reenactment. This was *happening*!

Emergency births happen all the time. On that note, be prepared to ditch your romantic view out the window and accept that this is all about getting mom and baby safely through the procedure, no matter what!

For dads, it can be a total onslaught. I came across three guys chatting about their experiences, and I had a good laugh, but you know what? It was also enlightening! Really, it's worth watching for some perspective and entertainment (Dude Dad, 2017).

Look, I can be a little squeamish, and the birth was not an easy time for me. But I endured as much of it as I could. Renee was a champ, I was a mess. However, I didn't want my daughter to grow up and be told that I was nowhere to be seen. Even if I fainted, I wanted her to know that I was a part of it all!

- **Cheat Code:** Pretend.

    That's right. A good friend gave me this advice after he went through a particularly tough ordeal. You've never done this before, but your partner is looking to you for support, so even though you're freaking out on the inside, try and be calm and brave for her. Use those breathing exercises from prenatal classes for *yourself*!

Before I knew it, a tiny cry echoed in the hospital room.

The Awkward Miracle of Life

I cried.

Maybe it was nine months of pent-up emotions all coming out. The roller coaster was finally going. Maybe it was relief. Maybe it was seeing my baby girl for the first time.

You might be more of a cowboy than I am, and hold back the floodgates with stoic machismo, but I'm not afraid to admit that I can weep in a silly Disney movie. Whether you shed tears is not important. Being there is number one. Not being too afraid to hold the baby is right up there, too. Hiding any signs of disgust, confusion, or apathy will round out the scene. As men, we don't have the same bond as the mother of our child. It's common for new fathers to be perplexed or even a little detached.

One new father told me, "The whole nine months my wife was pregnant, it was just the idea of a baby. And then I was handed this tiny, living human being. 100% real and who I'm responsible for. It was exhilarating and terrifying at the same time" (Cummings, 2017, para. 11).

Another one remembered being left alone with his newborn daughter and thinking, "The nurses are leaving *me* alone with her? But I have no idea what to do!" (Cumming, 2017, para. 10).

Don't be hard on yourself if you feel this way. Moms have had the benefit of bonding with your child for nine months already, all while you were running around making sure everything was ready. You don't have to go in big as if you're filling a role in some poignant movie scene. Tiny gestures will do the job just as well.

For me, I just stood there, my baby's tiny fingers clasped around my finger. She was wailing her head off, but I just stood there, mesmerized by the miracle of life holding on to me. *This was a part of me...* echoes of Tyler in those cries, reflections of Tyler in those blue eyes. It's those small moments that begin cementing a bond that will grow over time.

For other dads, "kangaroo care" is another form of enhancing bonding. This means placing the baby directly on the father's bare chest, skin-on-skin. And indeed, this can have a strong effect, aiding in the overall process. Either way, as awkward as it may seem, any small touch helps you to get acquainted with your new role as a dad.

I had no real idea of what I had got myself into, but come what may, I was all in.

The Birth Essentials Kit

Whether you've just found out that you'll be a dad in a matter of months or the baby's arrival is imminent, there's no time to lounge about. Start preparing some items you're going to need for when it's go time. I've put a handy list together, so you won't have to worry about forgetting anything important at home! Scan the link and get packing!

Chapter 2:

You're in It Now!

*Parenting shouldn't feel like a competitive sport.
It's plenty challenging without any added obstacles.*
—Ariadne Brill

Before kids, life was different. There was time to do what you wanted. You could party when you could, play sports for hours, and sleep it all off! It was like a leisurely scroll through Pinterest. Now, as a new father, there's no time for all this incidental living. The channel has changed to a mad scramble reality TV show, starring you! If I had had any notion of a quick, fun ride at the amusement park pre-fatherhood, I was rudely awakened by the fact that I had just bought a lifetime ticket on one of life's craziest, longest roller coasters! There was no getting off now...

Many guys, like me, have this dreamy idea of spending the next year or so watching the game on TV with a baby sleeping in our arms. Or some perception that life carries on as it always has, just with a fun distraction of a kid to keep us amused. But those moments are only small windows of joy that we manage to grab between sleepless nights. The luxury of quietly sipping a morning macchiato gives way to glugging back any kind of caffeine in a cup, no matter how it comes!

Adapt or Die

One of the biggest shocks for brand-new parents like Renee and me was that it is not all about the birth. See, I had some silly idea that if we just survived the hospital visit, then we'd be okay and move right into our new roles as Mom and Dad. Life could go back to normal somehow with a small addition to the family. I had been told by someone not to let the baby dictate how things were going to be, but rather, ensure things were the other way around. It kind of made sense that a newborn with no words, no ideas, and no clue should fit into our world; our pattern of life.

I had put so much effort and focus into getting through the birth that by the time we got home, I was unprepared for what was to come: this small baby would *not stop crying*. The nurses had insisted on breastfeeding, and Renee was determined to be the perfect mother. So, for a whole night, she persevered. If the birth was a drama, then this was a *horror*!

With tears streaming down my face from lack of sleep, I called my mom at 7 a.m. in desperation. Two hours later, she arrived on our doorstep like a salesperson to tell us about the miracle of formula. What a game changer. We were sold! Renee, still reluctant to give up her dream of breastfeeding, took some convincing, but after two weeks, our baby girl was a full-time formula kid. She was happier with a full tummy, and we were happier just to get back a few hours of sleep. Now, I could ease some of Renee's burden and find a way to be more involved.

Were the nurses wrong? Did the hospital miss the mark completely? No, not at all. It just wasn't the right option for our baby girl at the time. She had feeding issues that required a different route. Like so many opinions, recommendations, statistics, and techniques, we had to find what worked best for *us*. Indeed, when it came to grandparents, neighbors, experts, and even Google, we realized that at the end of the day, we had to do what was best for us as a family.

Finding What's Important

Again, I'm a Millennial. I'm not ashamed of it. In fact, I'm proud of being part of a generation that bridged the gap between the Dark Ages of the ADSL '80s and the world of instant internet today. Avocado toast is an ideal breakfast, and I'm not afraid to do a bit of job hopping. We get a bad rap from those who've gone before us, calling us entitled and lazy. But there's always good with the bad, and for those who want it, there's always the chance to evolve and become better.

Maybe being a bit of a momma's boy and living at home so long didn't help me get as ready as I should have been to bring a baby girl into the world. I might have started off on the back foot with so many people telling me what I can't, must, and should never *ever* do as a new parent. I've had to learn to stand by my decisions, even when one of them truly rocks the boat. Trying to stand on my own two feet as a husband and a dad has not been a smooth transition, but you know what? It has made me stronger and brought us as a family closer together!

I think the birth was a shock for my mom. After Renee entered the picture, she was no longer the only woman in my life, and with our baby girl, it was like she'd been pushed back even further. It was hard for me to let go of the apron strings, too. But things were happening so quickly around me and moving in new directions that if I didn't rise up and make decisions, then our fledgling family was going to be smothered. And so by putting my marriage and my child above other things, it became easier to wade through this minefield of good intentions and find a genuine flow.

Marek Demcak gives such a great analogy on the nature of prioritizing:

> Becoming a parent, your "ocean" transforms into a half-dry river... To keep the water flow, the first thing to do is not to add more rocks to the river. Saying yes consumes time—brings more rocks to the river. Saying no creates time. Time is a precious resource. How do you want to spend yours? If your priority is your family, dedicate the time to them. If you don't spend time with your family or on activities that really matter, your family is not your priority—as simple as that (Demcak, 2022, para. 2–4).

Role Confusion

According to research (Watkins et al., 2024), men initially struggle to figure out where they fit into this whole fatherhood thing. With the new addition to the family, things have changed, and it can be confusing for guys to know their place. Not only that, it can be lonely now that the spotlight has swung off of you and onto the baby. One father admitted that "as a dad, you should not show weakness," while another just figured it was best to "try to battle it myself" (Watkins et al., 2024).

There are tons of books and lots of guidance from health professionals for new mothers, but when it comes to dads, they're kind of on their own. Even those who make the effort to be involved can be sidelined because the focus is all on Mom and baby. So, instead of a starring role as the hero of the story, you can become just another passenger, another audience member.

One new dad recalled that during his hospital and doctor visits, the staff had "the mindset of treating you like you're a bit of a tool," and they even joked that he was struggling (Watkins et al., 2024). Breastfeeding can be another sore point for guys as they yet again feel excluded from the experience. A lot of guys live under the false belief that women are all naturally mothers, while dads have to learn all the skills. The truth is that both have to learn, even if it sometimes comes more easily to one of them.

And when it comes to fatherhood, there is often more confusion as to what is actually *expected*. Choosing between the more traditional breadwinner role and the modern hands-on approach can be tough. In the end, many guys find themselves in a tricky balancing act of working hard while trying to spend time at home.

In short, it's not an easy transition. But remember that it's not going to be cut-and-dry, all figured out from day one. Transitions take time, and this one is a major shift into a new chapter that might take weeks, months, or even a full year before you find yourself in a comfortable role as father and husband.

- **Cheat Code:** Small chats.

    Voicing your fears and expectations is necessary, but sometimes it can be a lot, especially for guys who don't express themselves. Take small steps—it doesn't have to start as a big conversation or a therapy session. Start by telling someone where you are *right now*.

Feeling Kinda Blue

Tom Spencer shares his struggle of shifting into fatherhood:

> There were struggles around breastfeeding. It was really hot that summer. The lack of sleep. Maybe something about the permanence of being a parent? I just felt sad a lot. I remember my partner and me commenting on a day that neither of us cried. I remember putting her in a sling for the first time and being terrified that she had stopped breathing and I'd killed her (Cosslett, 2022, para. 2).

Tom didn't realize at first that he was suffering from postnatal depression. The baby blues were for mothers, after all, not fathers, right? He couldn't figure out why he felt flat, depressed, and lethargic. At first, he thought it was the sleep deprivation, but it went deeper. Insomnia, anxiety, flashbacks, and guilt all combined into one hole that he had no way of climbing out of.

The truth is that for one in ten men, the reality of postpartum depression is a reality (Cosslett, 2022). Dealing with the birth, the added responsibilities around the home, and suddenly being in second place to a newborn are all very real burdens that can become heavy weights, enough to drown any man. One father admitted to still dealing with the "trauma of his son's birth five years ago, but his wife and his mum just tell him to get on with it, to stop complaining and be the man of the house" (Cosslett, 2022).

Fortunately, I am a bit too open at times. I find it easier to talk about my problems, but even for me, after the birth, there were moments where I just sucked it all up because that's, what I thought, was expected. Only later, when these thoughts were plaguing me at 1 a.m., did I realize that I had to express what I was going through, otherwise, they were going to cause issues down the line.

Elliot Rae's wife suffered from postnatal depression, and at the same time, he had PTSD due to witnessing the complicated birth of their baby girl. It took him a long time before he came to his senses, confessed what he was going through, and received the necessary mental care. Looking back, he had this to say:

> I wish I was a bit more prepared for the birth not to go to plan. I wish I had been more open to help from family earlier on. I also wish I knew about the prevalence of mental health problems with new dads and that it's OK to seek help. This would have meant that I would have sought help much sooner and could have prevented some of the challenging moments (Rae, 2022, para. 12).

Another new dad, Jordan, hid behind his busy work schedule or other distractions instead of recognizing he was spiraling. He thought this was just how it was—a numb reality of trying to exist. It took him a long time before he could admit his struggles. He describes it like this:

> I didn't cope for a long time because I didn't even recognize the issue. I isolated myself, telling friends and family I was "too busy" to stay in touch. But even in my isolation, I didn't make time for myself. I numbed out with YouTube, politics podcasts, and tech reviews—anything to avoid my own thoughts. I stopped working out regularly, telling myself I didn't have the energy. I wasn't a better partner, promising I'd get to it... eventually. I thought it was temporary. But it wasn't. It became the new normal. When my wife asked what was wrong, I'd just mutter, "I'm frustrated," as if that told her anything she didn't already know. It was my excuse to be sad, or in weaker moments, petulant (Axani, 2025, para. 7).

Looking After Number One

Instead of backing off, I jumped into being a dad, feet and all. But I had no clue, and pretty much ended up drowning in exhaustion from running around after my own tail. It was all so different, and I was on the verge of burnout. One piece of advice I did follow, though, was to find ways and moments to reboot. Just like in a game where your character loses a life, you can respawn and have another go at it. Luckily, there are some go-to hacks for grabbing back some time for yourself. They are as follows:

1. **Call out:** I didn't believe people could have zero time to cook or eat when they became parents, but I quickly bought into finding a healthy takeout option on my speed dial. Instead of gorging on junk food, I had a backup supply to keep us nourished and fueled.

2. **Vent it:** It's good to have a space to express yourself rather than piling on your wife. Create a social group on an app for your dad-buddies where you can share, laugh, and chat through your experiences.

3. **Turn off:** Sleep is the ultimate goal, even if it's for 15 minutes. I got into a habit of not letting distractions like phones or visitors ruin my chance to catch some shut-eye. Be strict about not bingeing or gaming all the time, as these do nothing to recharge you, only suck your energy reserves.

4. **Sweat it:** While sleep is what I wanted most, I knew I also had to keep active. Sports and other athletic hobbies here are lifesavers. The short bursts of exercise are excellent ways of releasing endorphins to boost energy reserves. I came back feeling pumped, ready for the next round of diapers and bottles.

5. **Zone out:** Instead of becoming a zombie, it's really good to meditate or calm down. Try yoga. I'm not very flexible, so for me it was just a contortion of stretches, but the measured

breathing really helped. Try mantras, read the scriptures, and dwell on positive input.

At first, these moments made me feel a bit guilty. I felt as though I should never leave Renee, always be on standby. But I had to learn that if I was not refueled, then I would have nothing to give. So really, remember that looking after yourself and having some me-time actually benefits your wife and kid.

You don't have to reinvent yourself and start doing things that are not you. Just think about what helped you unwind and relax before you had the baby, even if that means gaming! Trying new things can sometimes add even more pressure to an already difficult situation, so lean on what works for you *as a person*.

The Girl Dad Role Kit

Who *are* you anymore? Well, a dad is being everything to everyone all the time. It's a multitasking magic act that requires you to wear lots of hats. On that note, if you are going to survive the first week (and more), and not become a zombie, then check out this fun cheat sheet that will help you make the transition to fatherhood for every moment. Scan below!

Chapter 3:

Getting Stuck In

I don't have to prepare to be wrapped around my daughter's finger. I have been wrapped around her little finger since the day she plopped out into this world.
—Ryan Reynolds

No one bought me a cigar. I don't smoke for starters, and honestly, I didn't see the point in an old, meaningless tradition. Some guys have swapped Habanos for a pint of beer, using the birth of their kid as a reason to head to the bar and celebrate. Originally, this tradition actually stems from when a baby's head is sprinkled with water at a religious baptism. It was enough for Prince William to buy everyone a round at the Fountains Abbey pub, declaring, "Drinks are on me to wet the baby's head!" (Gard, 2024).

Some men still use the moment to puff away or slug back a few drinks, celebrating how tough it was for them. It must be said, guys will find *any* excuse to hang with their pals! To be fair, I'll admit to having a few strong ones, although it was more to calm my nerves than to celebrate! Looking back, I think maybe it wasn't so much to say well done for anything I had done up until that moment. It was more of a preemptive pat on the back for stepping into the shoes of becoming a girl dad. Those are not easy shoes to fill for any father—it demands a deeper love, a bigger sacrifice, and a lifetime of incredible moments.

If you are about to become a father of a precious princess, or you are already holding her in your arms, you deserve recognition and encouragement, however you decide to take it! Fatherhood is not for the fainthearted.

Unfamiliar Territory

For most men, the idea of having a baby is kind of like opening the door to a dingy basement. Just as in your typical horror movie, there is only a dim, flickering light and some squeaking stairs leading down into the dark unknown. Our curious nature drives us to find out what's down there, but only those with no fear and a death wish venture any further. Instead, the male instinct when it comes to babies is to close the door and stay in the bar or go straight back to work.

And, really, it's understandable. Men are not as instinctively bonded or used to handling squirming bundles of flesh. Alexis, a new father, gives his reasons for this common fear:

> We are scared of these creatures for good reason. Babies are tiny things that don't talk. They're fragile. Their hold on life is tenuous. And no one ever taught us what to do with them. No one taught us how to coo and rock, where to put our hands, or what the right way to hold a bottle is. What if the baby cries? What if I can't get the baby to stop crying? What will it say about me if I can't get the baby to stop crying? (Madrigal, 2013 para. 8–10).

A lot of guys still struggle with their own baggage of what they have perceived as parenting. This idea often comes from TV sitcoms or their own parents. And when role models are weak, dimwitted fathers like Homer Simpson and Al Bundy, or the oppressive Tony Soprano, it's no wonder that so many homes are plagued with high divorce rates. It's a sad truth that many new dads check out, thinking they don't have what it takes when faced with fatherhood.

Many men *want* to get involved, of course, but they end up feeling helpless when it comes to their newborn. They only find their purpose as a parent after many months have passed by—or even years! But by then, unsurprisingly, they have missed out on some of the best moments a father can actually give to a child.

- **Cheat Code:** It's not you.

> Don't take it personally if and when the baby cries or doesn't seem to want you. It's not choosing mom over dad, it's just acting on a womb relationship that has already existed for nine months. As with everything, it will take time, so just keep taking your place so the baby can get used to you in its life.

The Upside of Hands-on

If you want the best for your kid, then it's best to get in on the act early, right from the start. The benefits of a hands-on dad from day one are undeniable. Kids who experience a father's consistent presence during their first year have been shown to develop stronger self-esteem, healthier relationships, and more effective coping mechanisms later in life than those who don't (Silva, 2024). Just by soothing and calming a baby, a father teaches his young child to regulate and acknowledge their emotions. All in all, this consistent interaction teaches kids that they are understood and *loved*.

Neuroscience research (Silva, 2024) shows that when fathers actively bond with their babies, it helps develop synaptic connections in the little one's brain. This, then, enhances learning and emotional regulation later in life, helping them develop a better sense of security.

And if that's not enough, there is a reciprocal effect on the men who get hold, rock, and handle their small infants. Indeed, daily bonding is a transformative process that brings more happiness and fulfillment to fathers. Just as a person in general, empathy and patience were always qualities I had wanted to improve on, and luckily for me, the first few months of caregiving for my child presented me with key lessons in both.

Dads on Board

In past eras, men rarely got involved in their home life, especially when it came to baby duties. This was all relegated to the mom until such time as he could properly relate to his kids. It was customary to show up for the odd family photograph, but really, his job was to work and provide. Like a male lion, he strutted around while the lioness took care of the little ones, only letting them go near Dad when he was in a good mood.

Over the years, though, there has been a dramatic shift. Fathers are now way more involved. Millennials, especially, have taken this role much more seriously. 57% of dads today see being a parent as essential to who they are, spending three times more time with their kids compared to other generations. That's an average of eight hours per week dedicated to the baby as opposed to only 2.5 hours that fathers in the '60s gave to their kids. Just go online, and you'll see high-profile figures like Dwayne "The Rock" Johnson and John Legend at the forefront of dads taking their place in the home (Ea, 2025).

Sure, you may be petrified, out of your depth, and wishing you could just stay in the bar and drink the next few months away rather than clumsily holding a crying, pooping baby. But times have changed, and you are part of a proud new era of dads embracing the confusion and awkwardness with both hands and a full heart.

- **Cheat Code:** Be the go-to.

    You might not be able to breastfeed or do many of the other things Mom can, but that doesn't mean you're helpless. Get really good at one thing, whether it's diapers, bottles, or bathing. You'll not only become the person to turn to, but you'll feel valuable as well!

Good Connections

Bwoah!! Okay... So you've got this "thing" in your hands, holding it awkwardly like a football you'd rather pass off to a teammate! But this is a *living being*, not something you can use to score a touchdown. What on earth can you do to make the most of your time with a nonresponsive face? How can you connect with those two beady eyes glaring straight through you? In other words, what can you do to bond with your daughter at this early stage? How can you find your *girl dad energy*?

I tried a few of the following things and found that some worked, some didn't. Again, it's all trial and error as everyone is different and all situations are unique. It's up to you to find your groove, your flow, your rhythm as a father.

- **Skin-to-skin:** Human contact is number one; nothing else comes close to holding and stroking your little girl. It's the best way to bond as your baby gets used to your touch and smell. Babies have highly sensitive skin, especially mouths, cheeks, face, hands, abdomen, and feet.
    - If you stroke your daughter's palm, she will curl her fingers around yours into a grip because of a baby's grasping reflex.
    - Gently touch her cheek, and she will respond, using her mouth to explore in a rooting reflex.
    - Stroking your baby's back is very soothing when she's fussy and crying.
    - Gentle rocking is a great way to comfort and calm the little one.
    - Kangaroo care is a very powerful method of skin-to-skin.

- **Talk:** Before babies recognize faces, they familiarize themselves with sounds. So, holding some regular chats will enhance this. Your voice is one she will become used to, but will also use as a model to learn how to talk for herself.
    - You don't have to say anything too significant, just talk as if she can understand you. Tell her about your day, the latest sports results, about cleaning bottles, or the dinner you're preparing.
    - I loved sitting my little girl up to face me, and then talking to her like a little person who can understand everything I say. She listened intently, stared directly into my eyes, and explored my face with her little fingers.
    - You might feel a bit silly, but using a sing-song baby voice as you're talking is a winner. I always got a big smile when I asked her in a cutesy voice, "Did you do another poo? I think you did!"
- **Sing:** Singing is another important way babies learn about language and communication. It's also a great addition to your nightly bedtime ritual, as they enjoy the predictability of routine. And best of all, it's one of the best ways to stop the baby crying!
    - You can't go wrong with *Twinkle, Twinkle, Little Star*. If you're a little off-key like me, the good news is that babies don't really care about harmony and musicality; they just want to hear you. So, feel free to belt out a lullaby.
    - Use small actions to go with your song or incorporate a small dance.
    - Don't know any good songs? Make one up and sing about washing the dishes!

- **Play:** Before you get too excited, this is not the time to whip out the board games or fire up the Xbox. At this age, playtime can be intimidating since babies are mostly feeding or sleeping, and their attention span and responses are limited. The good news? This doesn't have to be a complicated, elaborate experience.

    o Tummy time is a great way to play, and all it really involves is putting your little girl down on her belly. You can use some high-contrast cards or a mirror to distract her, making her lift her head and work her neck muscles.

    o Going on a house tour is always fun. Show her some photos, paintings, the windows—anything, really.

    o Go on a Nishkramana. A Hindu ritual, this involves introducing a four-month-old baby to the five elements: earth, water, air, fire, and space (the fire element is not necessarily a raging fire but maybe the sun or just something warm!). This tradition is a reminder that the child is not confined to the boundaries of the house.

- **Walkabouts:** Another great way to bond is to take your daughter with you as you move about the house or go for walks. A sling or front carrier is very handy here, as it frees you up a bit.

- **Read:** This may seem absurd since she can't understand anything at this stage, but it's actually a very important part of brain and language development, even as a newborn! Kids who are read to and spoken to know more words by the age of two than those who aren't (Heger, n.d.).

    o Don't worry about getting through the whole story at first, it's more about spending time together.

    o Board books have bright, contrasting colors with large pictures and often include rhythmic, repetitive language that helps make the story exciting.

- o Read slowly and use your best high-pitched voice with exaggerated vowels. It's called "parentese" and helps your baby learn language.

- **Mirror and mimic:** Later on, you're bound to get irritated when your kid copies you, so why not get a head start? Instead of just a fun game, this is important for your baby's social, emotional, and cognitive development. Babies observe, so by teaching them to mirror your movements, they're experimenting and learning.

    - o Making funny faces by sticking out your tongue or doing a silly smile are perfect for your little girl to try and follow suit.

    - o Funny sounds are another way to have fun with your daughter. Animal sounds, songs, car noises, and funny laughs are great for her to try and copy and learn basic language skills.

- **Dozing off together:** You may be tired, and maybe you just want your own space, but why not combine that power nap with some bonding? I was always petrified I'd roll over in my comatose state and squash my baby or see her roll off the bed. Thankfully, that's why there are some safety guidelines in certain regions to avoid these exact types of things from happening. At nap time, for instance, I would put my daughter in the bassinet so she could still see me through the mesh on the side when she woke up. It's a win-win!

The Long Game

As inexperienced and totally out-of-my-depth as I was, I still gave being Dad from day one my best shot. I'll be honest, though, there were many days (and long nights) when I wanted to bail or just hit pause for a bit. It wasn't easy. Added to the sleepless chaos, I was faced with a baby who felt like she was already a tempestuous adolescent. She would be content one minute, then bawl her head off and scream at me the next. I never knew what to expect or what the fuss was about.

Truly, I felt as though I had been dropped into a battle with nothing but a toothbrush. I had no clue who the enemy was, and those who were supposed to be friendlies fired shots at me. The map I had been given looked like it was for another drop zone. And as much as I wanted to do my best, I just felt like curling up and crying! No wonder Marine Corps Capt. Joseph Tortorici, a father of six kids, tells any new dads that parenting is an "adventure" (Bustamante, 2022).

Look, you might not get it right from day one, and you certainly won't get it right every time. But the thing is, bonding with your new daughter should not become a pressure and a burden. It should be a journey where you both *find each other*. A few generations back, mothers and fathers were told that it was crucial to spend lots of time with the newborn during the first few days to establish an immediate bond. But lots has changed since then, and people have realized that bonding tends to take place over a much longer period. After all, many parents who might have been separated from their baby after the delivery for medical reasons or those who adopted their kids later went on to develop loving relationships.

So, the lesson I learned? I had to not be so hard on myself. There were some battles I was going to lose (or get totally annihilated in), but I found out that if I stuck it out and kept trying, then I would still be there at the end, and hopefully, win the war!

- **Cheat Code:** Find the funny.

    One thing you lose from a lack of sleep and feeling overwhelmed is your sense of humor. When that's gone, parenting becomes a thankless duty. No one wants that, especially your kid! Try laughing at different situations, mostly the ones you have lost complete control of. It'll ease the tension and remind you that this whole thing is an adventure.

The Bonding Kit

What are you supposed to do with this new addition to the family? How do you engage with the baby? Relax, I've gathered a few cool, fun tips and tricks for you, and I've gone ahead and put them all on one handy cheat sheet. Scan below for your free dad toolkit printable!

Chapter 4:

"Extra"-ordinary Dads

A father is the perfect blend of superhero, coach, and friend.
—Jeannie Hund

If you've come into the role of daddy slightly differently than I have, don't discount yourself! My scenario might be different from yours, but in the end, you and I both have kids. That makes us *both* fathers!

I was there for my daughter from day one. But some guys don't have that luxury. They appear later in their kids' lives for whatever reason, taking up the title of Dad, and doing the best they can. Stepdads are a common feature in our modern society—just look at Matt Damon, Blake Shelton, and Antonio Banderas. These men all took on the task of raising kids who were not biologically theirs (Herenda, 2022).

For other dads, they were there from the birth of the kid, but because of a relationship breakdown, they find themselves co-parenting with their ex-wife. If that's you, then hats off for not throwing in the towel altogether. You're sticking it out for the sake of your kid, even if that means only seeing them every second weekend! Despite everything, your presence means the world to your little one, so keep it up.

There are so many other equations that have seen the traditional idea being transformed into new, different configurations: surrogate parents, foster or adoptive dads, same-sex dads, and even mentor figures.

It's not DNA, a surname, or even the amount of time you've been in the picture that counts. It's whether you step up and fill the role.

Filling the Role

Now, don't discount yourself simply because you find yourself in a different position than the one that is traditionally held. What matters in the end is whether you fulfill the basic responsibilities and commitments. At the core of fatherhood, you will find the three Ps:

- **Provider:** There are the basics you fulfill, like giving your kid a home, clothes, and food. But there's more. Financial safety and resources fall under the job of a provider. In this modern era, where job security is not what it used to be, the stress and strain on men to take on the mandate as the provider has become tough. Women have had to step in and share the load, but that doesn't take away the onus on men to provide, even if it's not strictly financially. They are also expected to give emotional and spiritual support to their kids. And this is a far deeper call than just bringing home the bacon!

- **Protector:** Keeping your kid safe from harm is very important, as you become the advocate for their well-being. It's not easy, especially since attacks come from so many angles: bullying, peer pressure, the internet, accidents, and anyone or anything that wants to hurt your kids. As a shield, your job is to stop, or at least filter, the emotional or physical trauma of this world.

- **Permanence:** With the high divorce rates and many absent fathers in society today, this is proving to be a dying art. Being there for your kid consistently is a must in this world that is always shifting and changing. Establishing a steady presence through trust allows you to impact your child's life far into the future.

Roger Thompson explains what it means for a father to set up and be a real dad:

> Every dad sacrifices. The question is whether the sacrifice is coming from a well of love and willing sacrifice or from the grudging relinquishment of one of his conveniences. Every

father who wants to be a true dad will give up parts of his life, quite literally, for the needs of his children. Countless words in conversations and small acts of caring will build a bond and a legacy with each child (Thompson, 2022, para. 6).

So, if you find yourself as a new dad, an old dad, a bonus dad, or a half dad, what you make of the situation is up to *you*. Take whatever information and tips suit your scenario to help you adjust and rise to the occasion. There's no such thing as a perfect dad... There are just guys who are willing to do what it takes to see their young ones flourish. And that, my friend, is you.

- **Cheat Code:** Dad jokes.

    These are simply the best indications of real fathers. If you can't tell a dad joke, then learn. You may fail at diaper changing or making all the right decisions, but if you can't crack a lame joke that elicits groans and giggles (and a roll of the eyes from your partner), then it's going to be a very long (and boring) journey.

No Mistake, No Regret

Maybe you've found yourself here by complete accident. It wouldn't be the first time a guy was surprised to find out he's suddenly a father. Some men get a knock on the door 20 years later, finding themselves face-to-face with a grown-up daughter they never knew they had. Some stare at the pregnancy test thinking, %$#&!!!@. But, instead of avoiding reality and dodging the dad bullet, you can still step up and take your position.

Miguel Macia never wanted to be a father. He's quite open about that fact. It took him a long time to admit his regret about having a daughter. But rather than letting it become the theme tune for his life, he came to terms with the fact that it was okay to feel a loss for the childless life he wanted in order to embrace the new one he had.

This is how he explains coming to terms with his dilemma:

> I face my feelings of regret about having a daughter. I am able to contemplate them, allow myself to own it, and let it go. It doesn't consume me. I have come to understand that my abundant love for my daughter and the complicated feelings of regret I have around becoming a parent do not contradict one another. They both are true. And, though I can't be sure, I suspect that I'm not the first parent ever to feel this way. I suspect that others grapple with similar regret, though they may feel they can't express it. This might not be the life I once wanted, but it's the life I have, and there's so much about it that's wonderful. (Macias, 2024, para. 19).

Like Miguel, there are so many different circumstances out there, each dad facing his own situation, trying to figure it out. The reality is, if you're willing—even just a little bit—then there's space for you to grow and become the unique father you are meant to be.

The Girl Dad Step-Up Kit

Full-time, part-time, or bonus dad? You're still a dad, whichever way you look at it, so it's time to step up with confidence. Scan below for a sheet that will give you the courage and know-how to fill your role and remind you that *you count*.

Chapter 5:

Becoming Daddy

They tell you that at his age, all they do is eat, sleep, and poop. And what I've learned is that they can actually do all three at the same time. Who knew?
—Josh Duhamel

Everyone warned me, but I didn't take them seriously. After a while, you hear the same things so many times that you kinda block it out and just smile and wave! I was hit from all sides by people's well-wishes and cheeky cautions. The funniest were the ones from my friends who didn't even have kids yet. Everyone's an expert!

- "Your life will never be the same!"

- "You're going to be shattered..."

- "Wait till she starts walking, you won't keep up."

- "You won't have money or time to do what you want anymore!"

- "Oh man, how you gonna cope with a girl?"

- "She'll steal your heart, watch out!"

- "Hope your marriage survives!"

As much as I heard it all, I was still caught off guard. The sleepless nights hit me like a train. Trying to become a master at diapers was a nightmare. Renee and I hardly saw each other. It all came true like a predictable horror movie. But the one that really surprised me was how this little baby wormed its way into my heart. A little grin here, a coo there, and soon she had me... I had fallen for my princess!

Fathers and Dads

Being a biological father is one thing, but becoming a daddy is a totally different ballpark. One is an act of nature, something that is celebrated with cigars and bragging rights! The other is all about nurture, hours of invisible chores, encouraging words, quality time, and being a shoulder to cry on or a knee to sit on. Two complete opposites of the spectrum, or as Martin Cortijo puts it, "Anyone can be a dad, but not everyone can be a father" (Chow, 2016).

Unfortunately, most men fall into a category somewhere between nature and nurture. They end up just being fathers who show up when necessary: robotic providers. It's admirable, it really is. Giving your kid a roof over her head, food on the table, clothes to wear, and an education means you are ticking all the boxes. To stick it out despite all the challenges is worthy of a medal and a Father's Day mug.

But there is so much more to being a daddy; someone your kid will look up to and love dearly. It's not simply a "Once upon a time" a baby girl arrived, and the next you're walking her down the aisle so she can live happily ever after with her husband. The difference between an absent father and a hands-on dad is the hours of time spent making sure that the kid gets the best. That doesn't just include typing away on a laptop in an office so that the lights can stay on and the fridge can be full. It means filling the gaps in the home, changing diapers, cleaning bottles, and being present.

I remember briefly thinking about trying to stop the roller coaster, just enough to catch my breath. I was still trying to catch up on extra sleep without the added demand to be a hero! But this is what I had signed up for, so there was no turning back now…

Feed, Change, Repeat

As I rubbed what felt like 100 grade sandpaper out of my eyes, I vacantly stirred my umpteenth cup of coffee. Multitasking was the new norm. Instead of enjoying the sunrise with a brew of freshly roasted Colombian beans, it was just another caffeine kick to get through the next few hours of dawn. Only after the second or fourth gulp, my mouth screwed up in revulsion. This was not milk I was tasting, it was formula! I was too tired to get annoyed, too exhausted to laugh at the mistake, too far gone to bother making another cup...

The life of a new parent is a strange irony. It promises joy, but instead delivers in spades of fatigue. Watch a couple with a baby, and the telltale signs of hanging on by their fingernails are just beneath their beaming pride. While it's a rough ride of sleep deprivation, it's worth it in the end. Fortunately, there is an autopilot button that you can push when you're just too tired to think (or care). Setting up a basic system or routine can help guide you through the endless conveyor of bottles and poops. With endurance, a flexible routine, and a few hacks, the dreaded 2 a.m. shifts become bearable.

Search for Clues

Find what works for you as a couple and for your baby. Adopting someone else's rigid routine can backfire and take a long time to undo. Forcing a schedule on yourselves won't leave room to breathe (or laugh). Like building a puzzle, first look at all the pieces and see what works together to make the best picture. As a family, you are growing together on this journey.

- **Baby's Cues:** Paying attention to your daughter's hunger cues, tiredness, or overstimulation will help you to figure out when and how to respond. Sometimes, forcing a baby to change their instinctive circadian rhythm can be counterproductive. This doesn't mean bowing to every whim and whimper your little girl has (that will come later when she is 15!). Take the hints she gives and work with them.

- **Your Style:** What works for the neighbors (and for your own parents) won't necessarily be a match for you and your partner. You are a unique combination of cultures, values, and personalities. As hard as it is, don't compare yourself, but find what works for what you want as a family.

- **Other Options:** Before disregarding everyone else because you want to be unique, be open to trying different techniques. Your mom's advice might just be what you need to help the baby sleep better. That YouTube tip could be the very key to peace in the house. You're not failing if something doesn't work—like a scientist, you're searching for the right mix.

- **Be Patient:** The first few months can be tough. Like a boat out at sea, you have to navigate, use the sails at the right time, and adjust to the currents. You don't jump ship or try to ditch the boat for another one, after all! Use what you have and who you are. Push through, and soon you'll have a gap where there's smooth sailing for a bit!

Following Patterns

Whatever routine you create, it should incorporate these key factors:

- **Feeding:** This will be the dominant theme for the first few days and weeks. Whether it's breast or bottle, your baby should feed every 2–3 hours, or if she is rooting, sucking on her hands, or getting fussy.

- **Sleeping:** The good news is newborns generally sleep a lot, around 15.5 hours in a 24-hour period (LoRe, 2025). At first, your baby's pattern can be unpredictable in the beginning, but from about 6–8 weeks old, a bedtime routine can be established. Create a calm atmosphere to help her wind down for the night—even though she's tired, she might resist it. Prepare everything you need before you go to sleep so the night shift feeds will be easier.

- **Playing:** This should be a highlight for both you and your baby. Make these stimulating by being hands-on with tummy time, sensory play, and age-appropriate toys. Try to avoid having these moments just before bedtime.

- **Changing:** While a dirty diaper can catch you when you least expect it (sometimes moments after you've put a new one on!), they predictably occur every 2–3 hours. Be on the lookout for a tell-tale smell or baby becoming uncomfortable, as these usually indicate it's time for a clean.

- **Bathing:** To start off, don't make this too stimulating and wild, as you don't want to frighten the baby. This should be a soothing time that acts as a precursor to the inevitable bedtime. Introduce soft bath toys as time goes on.

Remember, these are just patterns to follow, making life easier in the first few months. The key to enjoying this time is remaining flexible. Your precious routine will be upended and sabotaged by many unexpected things. Just stay calm and don't force the issue. Learn to roll with it until you can get back on track.

- **Cheat Code:** Get it delivered.

    We were swamped with trying to stay awake and on top of things. Groceries were the last thing on our minds, and going out to the store would have pushed us over the edge. Having all our essentials dropped off at the doorstep saved us so many times, especially things like diapers and formula!

Daddy's Little Girl

If it wasn't tough enough to take my place and fulfill my duties, I had to adjust to being a girl dad. For so many years, men were given charge of rearing boys while girls remained in the kitchen with their mothers, learning, well, *girly things*. But over the last few decades, the male-dominated society of our grandparents has shifted to one where women are seen and admired for who they are.

It has become more common, more cool, and more necessary for fathers to take more of a role in their daughters' lives, especially after the late great NBA star, Kobe Bryant, proclaimed, "Girls are the best. I'm a girl dad" (Reilly, 2021). It's still not easier for men to suddenly adapt and bond in this way, but the rewards are incredible. As John Sinor once said, "It is admirable for a man to take his son fishing, but there is a special place in heaven for the father who takes his daughter shopping" (Parkerton, 2023).

Brian Molitor puts it like this:

> Our daughters' lives are not fairy tales with prewritten, happy endings. The threat against each of them is real, and the ending of the story is yet to be decided. In fact, the challenge is so great it will take a hero to save the day. A hero called . . . father (Molitor & Molitor, 2007).

So, I was a father... I had done the deed, produced the offspring. I had even survived the first few months and managed to keep the baby alive! But now, I was faced with the dilemma: Would I be a good enough king/dad/hero for her? There was going to have to be more than changing diapers and bottle feeding going on here if I was going to make the cut. There was more required if I had any hope of still being an integral part of her life when she was 18 years old. There was more than just showing up—it was going to require some meaningful engagement.

As a positive male role model, you're setting your girl up to become the best version of herself in life. According to studies (Gordon, 2023), girls with good, close relationships with their dads show less inclination to get involved in alcohol, drugs, and sex when they're young. Their emotional stability and self-esteem are far better than those who have difficult or distant fathers. These girls grow up to have healthy relationships of their own, achieve better academically, and are more resilient and level-headed (Porter, 2023).

For me, it was a no-brainer to give my all to my daughter, not just because I wanted to give her the best, but because there was a gentle yet very definite tug on my heartstrings. Instead of rough and tumble, slap on the back, spit, and peeing standing up, a world of pink tutus, period pains, chick flicks, and cheesy love songs awaited me. If this were an adventure, and I was going to be a hero, then I would need to learn to unleash every girl dad trick and power I had.

What's the Difference?

"Babies are babies. Whether they are a boy or a girl is not a concern to them and needn't be to us, either. Babies love to be cuddled, to play, to be tickled and to giggle, to explore and to be swooshed about" (Cassidy, 2023).

But you don't have to be a doctor or a biologist to see that a girl and a boy aren't exactly the same. As a girl dad, you have to be careful to always wipe backward to ensure no mess gets near her genitals. For boys, it's the other way around. That little difference should tell you something right from the start.

Society has done a bit of a backflip on genders. More guys are choosing to wear pink and look after their nails, while more girls want to compete in male sports like football and baseball. Without getting into a debate on the sexes and equality, the fact is that physically and emotionally, there are some distinct differences here. In short, knowing the science of how boys and girls develop and function really helps us to look after and raise them.

Psychologist Anita Sethi refrained from gender-stereotyped toys for her son and daughter, allowing them to develop their own identities. In the end, her boy made a race car out of his crib, and her girl became obsessed with shoes. Anita says, "Many of the differences we see are evident from birth, and may even be hardwired" (Sethi, 2025).

Here are a few of her general observations based on research, which could prove helpful when interacting with your brand-new daughter:

- **Imitating:** More than boys, girls excel at mimicking, so engage in this type of fun interaction.

- **Fine-motor:** Girls are quicker at manipulating toys and utensils, and later, will write sooner than boys.

- **Listening:** Shake a rattle and you won't see the difference. But talk, and you'll notice female infants respond far more than boys.

- **Face-time:** Girls respond more to eye contact and expressions than boys do.

- **Talking:** No surprise, but little ladies learn the gift of the gab sooner, using it more prolifically.

Watching and Learning

John Jimenez, a firefighter in LA, realized things had to change after he had a daughter: "Now I'm more conscious of what I say and how I behave" (Gordon, 2023). Kids watch everything, even from a young age; they're taking it all in. If you shout, stay calm, swear, slouch on the couch, or smile every day, they're analyzing each and every move you make. Whether you like it or not, your baby is taking mental notes, studying your behavior, and basing how they will behave and speak on what you do and say.

Under this continuous scrutiny, these three areas are the most important:

- **Eyes:**

    Do you pay attention to your daughter? She may be only a few months old, but she will learn from a young age whether you listen and acknowledge her. Eye contact, even with a baby, builds a strong connection and a sense of trust. Your eyes reveal what you're really thinking and what you're really feeling, despite the words coming out of your mouth. By giving her your full attention, she is learning that she is worth your time, valued by you, and, well, *special*.

Get down to her level, engage with her. Let her see and feel what she means to you through the way you look at her. Not only are you bonding with her, but you are also molding an image of the type of man she will one day marry! If you're like me, you want her to date someone who is attentive, not emotionally unavailable, too busy, detached, or on their phone.

- **Mouth:**

    How do you speak to your daughter? She might only respond with gibberish at this point, but what she is hearing is vital to her as a person. Even the way you speak to your wife is important. If there is criticism, verbal abuse, shouting, or other degrading speech, then your little girl will take that as the norm. It will affect her self-esteem growing up, and she will probably not choose you to confide i

    No matter how young, every girl wants to be told that she is beautiful, precious, and loved. Begin practicing if you're not used to expressing yourself by complimenting her whenever you see her. Words are like building blocks or wrecking balls, so choose wisely when it comes to your daughter.

- **Hands:**

    Being in the same room is great, but your daughter craves contact with you. Soft touches, hugs, and a stroke of her hair let her know that you love her. It doesn't even have to be continuous contact. If you are hands-on and engaged, she will get the message, too.

    You might be uncomfortable with being tender at first, but with practice, it will become more and more natural. Heavy or angry hands only send the wrong signals, so if you're angry, take a breath and calm down before doing or saying anything.

If you're not accustomed to such intimate, soft approaches, you're not alone. Men tend to avoid getting too personal and prefer letting a beer or a sports game do all the talking. But, as I learned, my daughter needed me more at an early age than I realized, and putting off engaging with her until I was comfortable wasn't going to do either of us any good. It took some practice (and feeling a little self-conscious) at first. Speaking in a silly voice, getting down to her level, and giving the baby my time was all a sacrifice that has been paying off ever since.

- **Cheat Code:** Find Your Thang.

    Focus on one aspect of your baby's day. If it's mealtimes, make it your time together. Starting my daughter off on solids, I had fun making sounds and saying, "Here comes the airplane!" It could be the way you change diapers, bathe her, or sing to her. She will look forward to those moments.

The Out-of-the-House Survival Kit

Keen to get out of the house and introduce your little girl to the world? Hold on there, cowboy! Are you forgetting anything? Probably... Best to scan below and find a simple diaper bag checklist I've put together for you. No dad should be stepping out into the Wild West unprepared!

Chapter 6:

Screwing Up (Again!)

> *Fathering is not something perfect men do, but something that perfects the man.*
> —Frank Pittman

It's a long way down from hero to zero.

Just ask Anakin Skywalker, Jean Grey, or Harvey Dent! They started off well enough, fighting for good, saving the world, and everything else that comes with it. But each of them lost their way, and in the end, Darth Vader, Dark Phoenix, and Two-Face became some of the most infamous villains out there! Dads face the same dilemma: One day you're the GOAT, and the next you're nothing more than an old goat. You try too hard, or you just give up. Living up to all the expectations and demands of society, parents, and yourself can be a tough burden to carry.

I know, trust me. I tried hard until I cracked. Just fulfilling the smallest tasks of hurriedly cooling down the boiled water to put into the bottles (because I'd forgotten to prep them) in the middle of the night proved too much. I felt as though I was failing. I was nowhere near being a hero (I don't have a six-pack or red underpants, for starters), but I had no intention of being a wash-out. So, where did that leave me?

The good news is that there is a third option, one between unattainable and deadbeat. Robert Downey Jr. (Iron Man himself) said, "Do I want to be a hero to my son? No. I would like to be a very real human being. That's hard enough" (Fernandez, 2021). I, too, reached a point where I realized that I didn't have to be a perfect dad to be a good dad!

Pressure to Perform

Imagine sitting and watching Michael Jordan playing for the Chicago Bulls or Tom Brady playing quarterback for the Patriots. Not only have you shelled out serious cash for tickets to these all-important games, but you've talked up your team on social media with your friends and everyone else who gets involved. There's a lot riding on the line. Maybe you even have your eye on the betting odds!

And then the worst happens: Michael and Tom just can't bring it home. Every time they fumble the ball, your stomach churns. How can these star athletes—who have excelled time and again—*fail*? How is it possible for them to let their loyal fans down so horribly? The crowd groans, throws down their drinks, and storms out, vowing never to support their teams... maybe until the next game! When Michael Jordan was asked about those moments, He had this answer: "I've missed more than 9,000 shots in my career. I've lost almost 300 games. Twenty-six times I've been trusted to take the game-winning shot and missed. I've failed over and over and over again in my life" (Patel, 2023, para. 3).

It's the same for fathers. The stands are filled with parents, grandparents, friends, brothers, uncles, neighbors, doctors, work colleagues, and every other nosy passer-by. They're all watching your every move, expecting you to come through as a winner. But like every fickle fan, they're also quick to shake their heads and tell all those willing to listen how they could have done it better! The moment you drop the ball, they're all over you with disappointment. And if they aren't, then it's you, beating yourself up.

If you want to appreciate the pressures of being a modern-day father, just look at these numbers:

- 72% say fatherhood is more challenging now than before

- 78% worry whether they are "good" fathers

- 77% say their stress levels are higher than normal

(Taylor, 2024)

Wesley is not a sports star or a superhero, but his morning with his daughter, Mila, reveals the pressure dads are under:

> She wants to watch Frozen for the tenth time, and while I really want to say, "No, let's do something educational," I find myself sighing and putting the movie back on. In the meantime, I'm trying to answer a work email with half an eye and ignore the chaos in the house. Well, the "perfect" dad in my head would have handled this situation better. He would probably do puzzles with her or come up with a super creative game. But me? I just fail miserably at times like these, and sometimes that frustrates me immensely (Perspective, 2024, para. 3–5).

Even though you just want to do your best, the reality is you're going to trip, fumble, maybe even score an own goal along the way, and let your team down. It sucks, but you're only human! Michael Jordan is still a hero, not because we remember all the games he lost or the shots he missed, but because we remember that he *showed up* after a string of defeats to win again!

- **Cheat Code:** Be Jack Reacher.

> Reacher is a fictional hero who busts his way through every town, but he does have some pretty sound advice for tackling any situation, knowing it can go bad at any minute. If you want to be as kick-ass as him, then do what he says: "Hope for the best, plan for the worst… Never count on anything except surprise and unpredictability and danger" (Child, 2012).

Worst Fears

If you're about to become a dad or you are one already, chances are you've been dreading making some of the common mistakes all new fathers make. Maybe, like me, you've already turned some of your fears into nightmarish realities. Even worse, maybe you've committed these atrocities while someone was watching (like your mother-in-law!). Either way, these happen to a lot of dads!

- **Drop down:** Turning for a brief second, I heard that terrible sound, "wump"! My heart sank as I saw my daughter sprawled on the floor, bawling her eyes out. What had I just done? It's one of the worst fears and, unfortunately, one of the most common mistakes new parents make. To avoid your daughter from having a nasty tumble, Dr. Homme, an ER specialist who often deals with kids who have fallen, says, "The only really safe place for a baby is on the floor if you're not holding them" (Homme, 2022).

- **Run out:** Babies have a knack for trying to ambush you when you are least prepared. Always carry extra wipes or diapers, just in case... unless you want Amy's story to be yours: "I guess we'd run out of diapers, because when I got home, my husband had made one out of a maxi-pad, a dish towel, and the headband I use when I take off my makeup" (Dubinsky, 2022).

- **Heat up:** Microwaves make life so much simpler, except when it comes to warming up the baby's milk. You can end up with liquids unevenly heated with hot spots that can burn. Also, the risk of leeching plastic from the bottle is a reason to go old school and not cut corners. Another wrong move is to not check the bath water, or to assume it's okay by testing with your finger. The way to assess heat is by dipping your elbow in or using a thermometer. The best temperature for a newborn is 98.6°F/37.5°C (Iftikhar, 2020).

- **Turn down:** I was not keen on inheriting someone else's stroller. Another baby had lain in there, maybe puked on it. So, I bought a new brand-name one that would even make car enthusiasts envious. A month later, I hit an unforeseen cash flow problem after visiting the emergency room. While I had an overpriced pushcart in my house, I had to suck up my pride and ask to borrow money for diapers! Another dad bought an entire range of expensive bottles for his second kid because they worked the first time around. The problem was that his second-born refused to drink from them, only wanting the cheapest version! Point is, hand-me-downs are a lifesaver and not something to be waved away. Check out Facebook Marketplace or other online social platforms for great deals. Buying too much stuff—or just unnecessary stuff—is a mistake many dads make. Stick to the essentials of clothes, diapers, food, wipes, and a safe place for the baby to sleep. Take time figuring out the rest, after all, your daughter is going to outgrow it soon anyway!

- **Measure up:** This one will follow you all through your life as a parent, but it's most prevalent in the first year. Milestones are great because they give you a sense of what's coming and what to look out for. The problem is that not all kids (or parents) fit exactly into those parameters. Getting caught up on whether your baby is sitting at six months or not (especially since the neighbor's kid was doing it at five) puts huge pressure on you to perform. Constantly gauging and comparing yourself and your kid against the "norm" will exhaust and stress you out. So, use the milestones as a loose guideline and relax! Only then can you genuinely enjoy your kid growing up.

- **Hang back:** One of the worst mistakes dads make is thinking they're babysitting, looking after the kid until Mom gets back. It's an easy mindset to fall into since many guys feel like a spare wheel, a back-up, or a substitute, rather than a parent. But just filling in the gap means you're losing out on bonding, engaging, and enjoying time with your own kid. Here, distance does not make the heart grow fonder, it only creates a wider chasm between father and daughter. Get in there and own it!

There are many other mistakes dads fear (and often make), like not bonding straight away, puking while changing diapers, telling your kid to shut up because she won't stop crying, or forgetting your newborn somewhere! Despite all the handbooks, guidance, and warnings, mistakes will happen—even if you're Jack Reacher or Michael Jordan! It's what you do with those moments that determines whether you are growing as a father or not.

Losing It

A lack of sleep is enough to push you over the edge. Take away all your usual go-tos and replace them with a demanding baby, a grumpy wife, and the feeling that everything is falling apart... then stand back and watch. It's a ticking time bomb. If you don't hiss a curse word under your breath or snap at your innocent child for ruining your night, then you're a saint.

Again, I've cracked. Not once, either. I'm talking almost weekly, sometimes nightly! The pressure to perform, the constant treadmill, and the brittle moments Renee and I shared when we both thought it was each other's turn to take over, all added up. I may have said some things that I didn't really mean. And I may have stepped on some toes while I was at it! In short, I may have messed up in those heated moments.

Luke, a father of six, inherited his explosive anger from his own dad. He did his best to remain calm, bottling all his emotions up inside, but then he would let rip at the kids for the smallest things. It wasn't great for the home atmosphere, his marriage, or modeling behavior for his kids. He worked hard at finding ways to acknowledge and circumvent those stormy tirades. One trick he learned was to have a word he could say when someone did something daft or things went awry. In his words, "If someone's doing something that is making me mad, I will take a breath and calm it down a bit, but in my brain, I'll just be going, 'Interesting, fascinating'" (Healthy Male, 2024).

I found a great variation of Luke's, called the "Parental Pause." When you're about to explode, try these steps:

1. You stop moving. You ground your feet.

2. Gently bend your knees.

3. Place your right hand on your heart.

4. Take a deep breath. Maybe another two deep breaths.

Then you slowly stand close by or kneel near your child. Be present.

Be still.

Observe calmly the world through your child's eyes.

Inwardly – repeat these words silently:

"My child/teen is not bad or naughty – they are just struggling to cope with their world. This is normal developmentally. Let me be what they need right now – a safe base."

That's it! (Dent, 2016).

Luke says it's not easy at first, but you can recognize and deal with these issues. As he puts it, "My advice to other dads struggling with anger is that it's ok to feel angry, it's how you express it that's important. I needed to learn that lesson. Don't be afraid of anger, make it work for you. That could be exercise, yard work, or writing it out" (Healthy Male, 2024, para. 12).

Dealing With Mistakes

Justin Brey was outed in the middle of church as the sacrament was being passed. When he didn't take communion, his kid asked a little too loudly why not. Instead of cowering in embarrassment, Justin explained that he'd made some mistakes and was showing how sorry he was. His son's response is one we can all remember when we mess up. Looking up at his dad, the boy whispered, "It's okay to make mistakes, Dad, I still love you" (Brey, 2023).

I don't know about you, but I struggle with guilt after doing something wrong or dumb. There's that gnawing feeling like I messed up, and there's no way back. That black mark against my name, because I'm a loser father who just can't get it right. Guilt is like a hook that just drags you deeper. The trick (if there is one)? To allow yourself to *feel* it!

Sounds contradictory, but when I pretend I'm fine or ignore it, it just gets worse.

1. **Accept:** Don't hide it or try to push it away, it'll just grow bigger! Guilt can be a sign that you know there's room for improvement, that you wish you could do things or be better. That's a good start because every dad is learning and growing to become better.

2. **Admit:** Be a man and own the mistake. Men can be really good at blaming others or ignoring what just happened. Instead of progressive, that's just backtracking. Moving forward from guilt is to take it on the chin and wear your mistake.

3. **Apologize:** A quick sorry might sweep it all under the rug, but all the emotions and damage still need cleaning up. Learn to express your regret and your willingness to try harder. Be sincere and don't overdo it. I've made a mistake and then made it even worse by profusely apologizing. A simple, sincere sorry is good enough.

4. **Absolve:** This is a tough one. Give yourself a break, you're only human. It's time to *forgive*. That's right, we often think that forgiveness is about letting others off the hook, but it's important to do the same for yourself, otherwise, you'll just carry the burden of guilt with you. Lay the mistake down—you can't change what happened, but you can learn, grow, and move on.

Lessons for Life

Instead of roadblocks, obstacles, or massive end-of-the-world catastrophes, mistakes can be the springboard to learning new skills. It's a complete paradigm shift, a growth mindset. Every mistake is an opportunity to evolve. As a new father, I was keen but way out of my league, and I made more than my fair share of blunders. I had two choices: slink into the shadows with a quiet whimper and lick my wounds, or continue on, stumbling boldly into heroism.

Embracing errors seems counterproductive and contrary. It took me a while to understand this, as it was really strange for me to see my mess-ups as a positive way forward rather than a backward wipe-out. But then I read about the long-term benefits of having a growth mindset. It turned out, it wasn't just for me… I was fostering resilience in my daughter! When she sees my mistakes and watches me figure out how to pick myself up and bounce back, she has the perfect example of tackling life with a positive attitude!

Dr. Tara Christie Kinsey of the Hewitt School in New York says this:

> When parents value their children's success over their character development, their children show elevated symptoms of depression and anxiety… Adults preach that children must try new things, bounce back from failure, and respond constructively to feedback. But what children need is for the adults in their lives to model that behavior (Kinsey, 2016, para. 8–9).

See, effort is worth more than success. As soon as you think you're an expert at something, you're about to learn a hard lesson and be brought down a peg. It's best to think of yourself as a willing beginner every morning. In the end, being the hero is great, so long as you're prepared to sometimes just be dad as well.

- **Cheat Code:** Celebrate the wins.

> Any chance I can get to tell myself I'm crushing it as a girl dad makes up for those days when I completely suck as a father and a human in general! Take the win and pat yourself on the back with a well-deserved beer. You might be the only one who saw you change that diaper in record time, so enjoy the self-applause!

The Resilience Kit

Want to ride in as a knight on a white stallion and save the day? That's admirable, but it won't happen every single time, sadly. You're going to fall off your horse more than once! To make getting back up easier, I've created a plan to help you be more resilient. Scan below and keep on riding!

Chapter 7:

Three's a Crowd

A child is a grenade. When you have a baby, you set off an explosion in your marriage, and when the dust settles, your marriage is different from what it was.
—Nora Ephron

We were in love, Renee and I. We had a great partnership, really. And we wanted a kid. We were prepared, too—I had Googled everything about being a parent. We anticipated that things would get sketchy, but we were solid... and then the wheels came off.

Imagine a mobile, one of those things that hang above a crib, turning beautifully in the breeze from the open window, sometimes accompanied by gentle music. Well, that's your marriage. At first, it's a "husband and wife who are tied to each other by their heartstrings," bouncing around as they adjust and find balance. No sooner have they settled than a baby is added in. "New strings are added, the original ones are stretched, and the whole mobile wobbles crazily out of whack" (Stoop & Stoop, 2005). What makes it worse are the expectations of what your "mobile" will look like and how you think it will gracefully move through all the phases of life. But in reality, you're left with a lopsided mess of strings that could fall apart at any moment at the slightest gust of wind.

See, when the equilibrium is disturbed, the first thing couples do is try to go back to how things were before the change. But this doesn't work. In fact, it only creates more stress for the new parents. The truth is that with an infant in the house, there is no going back!

Out of Balance

Christopher, a new dad, shared my sentiments: "What the *$#!@*&! is going on?" His neat little world had been tipped upside down, and like me, he was left treading water, trying to stay above the tide:

> Our child is only two months now, but wow—it has been the most challenging two months in both of our lives. Our communication skills were par before, but now trying to juggle handling a newborn, we are both so focused on taking care of our daughter that we are not taking the time to communicate and work together to make this easier. We have a great marriage, but when you instantly reduce both of your average sleep times by nearly 75 percent, things change. You have to learn to work together again under stress, distress, and lack of sleep. We both wish we had more time to become prepared for this (Brown, 2021, para. 9).

Renee and I were so busy, so tired, that any time for ourselves seemed like trying to get a person on Mars. Indeed, it felt as though we had been shot up into space only to end up floating, untethered between Earth and our destination. I didn't want to end up with a broken mobile, missing one or more of its pieces. I was in it to keep my marriage intact. But splitting myself between husband, dad, and businessman was a tough circus act. It was like a combo of a juggler, clown, sword-swallower, tiger-tamer, and ringmaster. I didn't know how to walk the tightrope while keeping all these other roles from crashing to the ground!

Everyone gave us suggestions and opinions, even our friends who had no kids of their own! One group followed the idea that by doing everything for the baby, the relationship would follow. The others, in contrast, recommended the complete opposite: Do everything for the relationship, and the baby would be fine.

In the end, we opted for "a little bit of both," something Dr. Nicole Pernod, a renowned psychologist, suggests for all expectant parents (Gannon, 2023). If you focus too much on the baby, your relationship can suffer. Spend all your time on your marriage, and you miss out on what your baby needs for development. This is a tough act to get right even when you have a full eight hours' sleep every night, no unreasonable expectations, or anyone relying on you 24/7. It helps to have a few tricks, of course, so that you don't end up as another has-been three-ring circus!

- **Cheat Code:** It's normal.

    Using rational statements, you can bring some normality to your situation instead of trying to live up to high, unreachable expectations. "Being too tired for romance for a few months is normal." "It's typical for mothers to be more focused on the baby than on you at first." This takes some of the pressure off and helps you not to demand anything from your partner or feel like a let-down.

On the Same Team

We had to shift perspective. We realized that wishing things to go back to how they were would only end in frustration and resentment. As much as I wished it were just me and Renee sleeping in and sneaking a quick cuddle, it wasn't going to be like that for a long time. We were no longer just a couple—we were a *family*. This is a new chapter, so embrace it with everything it has to offer. Expectations need to die in everyday life. Too often, parents have an ideal of how it will be, and when reality smacks them in the face, it's fight-or-flight! But accepting your new existence is the first lesson in moving forward.

Working as a team is the most efficient way of dealing with the added pressures and demands that come your way. But no matter how much we played tag team, there was always a mountain of laundry, toys to trip over, and an aroma that smelled like baby powder and poop! We just became cranky with each other. See, when fatigue and stress kick in, an automatic selfish mechanism to stay alive at all costs kicks in with them. Not a great recipe for keeping the relationship alive, I'll tell ya.

Again, it came down to communication—sitting together and talking it through. It wasn't easy to keep our emotions out of it and not play the blame game, but we managed to highlight some issues that were hamstringing us. We had to reevaluate the way we were handling things, otherwise, we were going to take it out on each other. These were some of the issues that Renee and I had to sort out if we wanted to be a better team:

- **Gatekeeping:** I wasn't very good at certain tasks. It was great to have Renee's help, but she had to learn to step away and not hover, not always tell me how to do something, and not criticize me when I got it wrong. If you're going to learn to be capable, you also need some room to try, fail, and succeed.

- **Comparing:** Okay, I was guilty of this one. Telling her how bad my workday was when she was drowning in diapers, bottles, and cries was a surefire way to get the death stare. Score-keeping and tit-for-tat arguments over who changed more diapers, who did more shifts, or who stayed up the longest—none of these bring you closer as a couple.

- **Differences:** You're not going to do things the same way all the time. It's not a negative, and you don't need to be robots. Your different views and skill sets are what's going to form and mold your daughter into her own unique person, not a clone! Identify each other's strengths, recognize weaknesses, and accept that there will be different ways of getting to the same point.

It's normal not to agree on every single aspect of parenting. After all, you both come from slightly different backgrounds and have your own opinions on how things should work. That's okay, as long as you agree on the big things, the major rules. Don't let little irritations become big cracks. It's going to take some talking, trying, and testing to get on the same page. But it's worth it, as research shows that collaboration between parents results in kids who excel in problem-solving, feel more secure, are generally confident, and are less anxious (Vallerand, 2020).

- **Cheat Code:** Quick catch-ups.

    There isn't enough time to have long discussions, so five-minute chats can help to get you two on the same page. Just find out how you're both doing, share your day, your struggles, or whatever else is on your mind. It's better to have a quick outlet than to bottle it up and wait for a long, lengthy argument and/or therapy session!

Reigniting the Spark

So, you make a well-oiled, finely-tuned, baby-changing/feeding/comforting/playing machine. Well done! But teammates are just that—*teammates*. Before you know it, there's no more spark or chemistry, and you're thinking about signing up for another team. It happens more often than you'd think. Parents simply survive all the way through raising their kids, only to bow out at some point because they're no longer in love.

The problem is there's no energy left to create a spark. You've just been kicked in the wrong place again by your "cute" little kickboxer as you tried to change her diaper. Your brain is fried, and all you want is sleep. You'll easily get the audition for an extra in the next zombie movie! Shutting out the world and crawling into bed alone is all you want. It'll take a bolt of lightning to boost your love life. Date night is the furthest thing from your mind. What happened to "I'll love you for better or for worse, in sleeplessness and dealing with kids"?

Renee and I were locked into making it work and became task-oriented with barely any time for romance! There was no energy or time for sweet nothings being whispered in each other's ears. Conversations were more like "If you can change her diaper, I'll grab dinner!" It took a concerted effort to grab hold of the runaway train before it became completely derailed. And you know what? We began trying a few of these techniques and found a combination that worked quite well:

- **Time:** Grab a moment to be together, whether it's five minutes or an hour. Quality does not mean quantity. It's about turning the focus on your partner, giving her a moment of your day. It does not have to involve any physical intimacy. Just be together, share adult conversation, and connect. Don't put pressure on each other. Put on a movie, drink tea, have dinner, or fall asleep together. It doesn't mean leaving the house or moving the baby out—just find a space where you can be "alone."

- **Thanks:** You'll be surprised how far gratitude goes. Saying how thankful you are for your partner's help and sacrifice, even in small tasks, lets her know you see and appreciate her. Make a point of finding something, anything, to be grateful for. It won't just give you a more positive outlook on your situation, it'll also give you new eyes for your better half. Just those simple heartfelt words can be enough to blow life into smoldering embers!

- **Touch:** Without looking for it to lead any further, hold her hand, give her a hug, or rub her back. Try a six-second kiss. It doesn't have to be shooting stars and rainbows, just a fleeting reminder that you're still her partner and lover, not just a high-fiving, fist-punching, tag teammate. Try a head massage... You never know!

- **Turn off:** Phones, work, TV, games. Switch it all off so you can give your full attention to each other and enjoy the moment. Without the added interruptions, it becomes a bit easier to turn the volume of all your inner distractions down as well. You could even meditate or do some yoga together. Who knows what positions you'll find yourselves in!

- **Transfer:** Shift the weight off yourselves by outsourcing. It's time to cash in on everyone's threats to "help if you need it." To have someone babysit or look after your little one, you can find some time to breathe (if you're ready to "let go" of your little one, that is!). Or find the benefits of getting someone else to deliver food, cook for you, and clean the house once in a while.

- **Toast:** Celebrate the wins, no matter how small they are. Break out some bubbly (nonalcoholic if Mom is breastfeeding, of course). It's not just about recognizing that you both got something right; it's about acknowledging each other's efforts and role in getting there. Tomorrow may be a disaster, so enjoy the victory while you can. Those small stepping stones can absolutely unite you.

- **Therapy:** There's a huge stigma when it comes to couples going for counselling, especially from grandparents and parents. But it's not an indication of major mental or marriage issues; it's a proactive way to express, communicate, and order your life. For those who are struggling with postpartum depression (yes, remember that dads can also suffer!), finding a professional safe place to heal is important if you want to revive your relationship.

Between the Sheets

Alright, let's talk about getting your groove on. It's the big question on most men's minds… sometimes the only question! For guys, having to wait so long after the birth can be a real source of frustration and resentment. Normally, this means anything from four to six weeks of no intimacy, according to medical experts (Stewart, 2023). Your partner's body has changed, been put through the wringer, and may need some time to adjust. Some men may have to put off bedroom time even longer if there are complications. But looking at the long-term big picture, you have a lifetime to make up for this "short" pause!

For new dad, Julian, it came as a bit of a shock that he and his wife had to navigate. As he says:

> My wife and I are legitimately best friends. And we love spending time together and having romantic nights. When that

shifted for us, it was really hard. We went from regular date nights and sex three times a week to falling asleep during the opening credits to sex maybe once every few weeks. It was tough. We definitely felt further away from one another but also closer at the same time? It was a different type of romance. But if you understand that this is what happens—at least for a while—the connection you'll feel to one will be really strong. We definitely were prickly with one another and missed getting that time together, but once you understand that that happens, it'll make things easier (Brown, 2021, para. 8).

But just because you're both physically okay to get back into bed together, that doesn't mean it's what you both *want*. See, it can be hard not to take it personally, but you have to remember that there's a new person in the family, and Mom's attention and love can sometimes be more focused on your daughter, and not on you. It sounds so silly, but guys can get jealous of this little one taking away all their "fun."

If you're man enough to see past the baby "stealing" your thunder and not take your wife's hesitation to jump in the sack as rejection, then there are ways to pave the road to being together again. Sometimes, this new chapter turns out to be even better than what you both had before the birth! Here are a few soft touch techniques to make it work:

- **Courting:** Remember the flowers you used to give her, the little notes you wrote, and all the other romantic gestures? Well, it's like you're 19 again, trying to win your date's heart. Think of it as falling in love all over again. Make her feel like a woman, not a mother! And it doesn't have to end in sex... It's a long game you're playing here. Enjoy the chase!

- **Warming-up:** It's not just about the lead-up to intimacy. It's also about helping both of you relax and enjoy the moment again after birth. Take it slow, go gently, and focus on connection rather than "getting anywhere fast." After the birth, some women need a little extra help, especially if they're breastfeeding.

- **Explore:** Couple time is not just about the action; it's about everything else as well. Dr. Pernod suggests you could even spend the time "touching, stroking each other's hair or rubbing each other's feet (Gannon, 2023). See this as an opportunity to find those other sensual areas that can enhance your intimacy.

- **Anticipate:** Keep your expectations low, even though your body might be racing ahead of you like a buzzing teen. Don't be shocked if it's not working at first, or if it's a bit different. Also, be prepared for the baby to conveniently interrupt your lovemaking. They have a knack for timing!

- **Patience:** This is so important. Take your time and don't put pressure on your partner to suddenly perform. Her body may have changed a bit, and it might take some adjusting. Find a comfortable position and let her set the pace, not you. Slow and steady wins the race!

- **Talk:** Maybe not so much during bedroom time, but before and after. It's important and helpful to you both to figure out where you are and what works. Private moments together should be enjoyable for you as a couple, and only by being open can you find the best positions, maneuvers, and methods.

Again, physical intimacy is *not* a relationship. It's a beautiful *extension* and *expression* of one. So, enjoy all the other aspects, and you will find that intimacy again sooner than you think. But be warned, unless you want another baby hot on the heels of your first one, be safe! A woman can ovulate 45 days after delivery if not breastfeeding, but it can be sooner, so it's best to use some protection just to be sure (Stewart, 2023).

Looking after your wife is another way of looking after your daughter. If she is happy and fulfilled, then that radiance and love will be felt in the home. What better way to bring up a kid than in an environment of openness and affection? I enjoy hugs myself, and so I make sure to give Renee as many as I can in front of our little girl so she can learn what love should look like. And one day, hopefully, she will know what a healthy and loving relationship looks like and how men and women should treat each other!

Dr. Pernod sums this up best, saying, "You and your partner are the foundation that your child will rely on, and if you're strong, they'll have a firm ground to stand and grow on" (Gannon, 2023).

The Relationship Reset Kit

Feeling forgotten, left out, or sleeping on the couch? Being a dad and a husband at the same time is a real circus act, as we've covered. If reigniting passion is the last thing on your mind, it's okay. I've put together some great ideas for funky date nights that won't wake the baby and won't break the bank. Scan the link and get those embers glowing again before you know it!

Chapter 8:

Survival of the Fittest

> *A girl is innocence playing in the mud, beauty standing on its head, and motherhood dragging a doll by the foot.*
> –Alan Beck

I heard from so many people that I needed to enjoy every moment because it all goes so quickly. But knee-deep in diapers, rocking a wide-eyed baby while trying to find a sterilized bottle at 2 a.m., the hours and days just blurred into one long, dark tunnel. It was like getting stuck on one of those game levels, running round and round without finding the secret porthole. Someone had left our new life on repeat...

It was only around the seven or eight-month mark when we finally came up for air. Our little cherub was finally "sleeping through." No sooner had our world settled than she got sick, however, and whatever semblance of routine we had developed went straight out the window again. And before we knew it, she was spitting bubbles on the one pink candle on her Elsa cake in an effort to blow it out. It was only after tidying up after the party that I had a chance to flick through the pics. Suddenly, I realized that she was no longer a baby...

Time always flies in retrospect!

Milking Every Moment

Posting pics of the baby each month is the trend on social media, especially if you have a unique, heartwarming, or funny caption to go with them. It's not just a boast to the world but also serves as a vivid reminder of your journey as parents. It's important to hold onto these memories and enjoy the milestones as much as possible because, well, your daughter will never be that small again—*ever*. Before you know it, you're standing at the door ready to face off with some lame excuse for a boyfriend who wants to take her to prom.

Your baby's achievements are all wonderful, especially if you're there to witness them. All the firsts are magical moments worthy of videos and bragging rights.

- That smile, a little toothless grin to melt your heart.

- An infectious melodic laugh that makes any day better.

- Crawling on all fours, even if it's squirming like a turtle.

- Sitting up without falling over (kind of...).

- That first word you hope will be "Dada," just to prove you're her favourite.

- And, of course, the moment she walks... and then falls over!

Remember, don't put any pressure on whether she's reaching all these achievements at the "right time" or not. Babies figure these things out in the end, and some take their time while others race ahead. No college application asks when she first talked or walked! There are so many incredible growth points in a baby's life, but what if you miss those pivotal moments? What if you're not there when she totters around or babbles something for the first time?

Bwoah!! It happens. I missed a few of them myself, and I really beat myself up about it. That is, until I learned to enjoy whatever first moment I was there for, even if it was an unconventional one! So, for those dads who can't rush home from work to witness the miracles, look out for these other great filming opportunities:

- The poop in the bath is not one every dad wishes and waits expectantly for, but when it happens, you can't forget it!

- The second word is a great follow-up to the first one. It's often a funny indication of what she's interested in, like "dog," "eat," or the feared, "No!"

- The first dance is far more entertaining than her wobbly first steps. It's a combo of chubby arms moving, little body bopping, and joy on her face!

- Along the way, she'll suddenly find a friend, her very first!

- That toy or thing that she won't give up is so precious, and sometimes she won't sleep without it!

- "Sorry" will break your heart when you hear it from her lips for the first time. Unfortunately, it will only happen after she's broken something valuable!

- Later, you might get to hear her crack her very own joke. When she says something funny, it'll bring the house down.

Becoming a Little Person

There are going to be so many moments, and you will get to be part of many of them, so get involved. Teaching her to ride a bike (or scooter) and getting her to swim are some of the best times she will have with you, even if they involve some tears along the way! Here are a few ideas to allow your little girl to become her own person and learn new things:

- Let her dress and feed herself.

- Take her on a bus or train.

- Go to the zoo, library, or supermarket.

- Build sandcastles on the beach.

- Teach her simple safety rules, like crossing the road with mom or dad, not touching hot things in the kitchen, and not playing with electric gadgets.

This is also the time when you can become her BFF! Ditch the bravado man act and get down to girlie time. She'll be begging to have you as her playmate in any of the following:

- **Tea Party:** Get out the plastic china set, make those delicious mud cakes, and enjoy spending time with other guests like Teddy and Dolly.

- **Manicure:** Extend your fingers and watch her do wonders on your nails as she smears different colors about.

- **Make up:** Why not go the extra mile and see what she can do armed with lipstick, blush, and other cosmetics? (Remember to take selfies!)

- **Dress up:** You don't have to don a pink tutu (although it'll be a memorable occasion if you do), but you can be a pirate, cowboy, or wherever your own childish fantasies lead.

I found that my daughter became so much more receptive and responsive as she entered her toddler years. As she moved into the next phase of her life, I could see the extra effort from that first year paying off big time.

- **Cheat Code:** Hairdos.

    Ponytails, clips, and braids are trickier than they look. If you learn to do at least one style, you'll avoid many tears.

Self-Preservation

There should be an exam to pass before becoming a dad. Something like Navy SEAL training, where you learn camaraderie in hardship, overcoming fatigue, and staying fit. But the truth is, anyone can become a dad... even *you*! No requirements. It's why lots of fathers find themselves a sorry picture of what they used to be before the birth.

So, as you crack open a cold one to celebrate getting through year one, it's hard to hide the fact that although everyone survived, everything else has gone to the dogs. There's a slight bulge around the belly, love handles sag over the boxers, and there's nothing left in the tank. You've got a Dad Bod, and you're completely spent. However, with a little training and discipline, it's possible to not only scrape through but come out on top after your first year as a father (and maybe even have some abs and pecs to show for it!).

Physical

Me? I had very little time (and no energy to begin with). The shorter the workouts, the better! The only time I found for fitness during the first few months was between shifts. After a week or so, I could feel extra reserves fueling me up as my body responded to the exercises. I opted for an all-around cardio and fitness workout every day: 6–10 reps of push-ups, 6–10 reps of lunges, and 6–10 reps of mountain climbers. Okay, I skipped a few days in between, but at least I tried!

Pilates is great for core muscles, especially when you realize how much bending, twisting, and reaching you're required to do with a newborn at home. You could even include your baby in your regime, using her as a weight! To break up the monotony, squeeze in a bout of boxing, a jig of dancing, or a quick heart-stopping jog.

If you're like me, not so much into fitness or trying to look like an Adonis, then you might need the added motivation of enrolling in a fitness class at your local gym. You owe it to yourself and your family!

Dan, a new father, managed to sneak in exercises with his partner:

> My wife and I found that follow-along YouTube videos like HIIT or circuit sessions were a great way to exercise together. We both felt guilty or selfish for leaving the other to exercise. So, exercising together with the baby was the best solution! (Redmond-Fisher, 2022, para. 9).

Mental

Before you lose it entirely, be sure to step out of the chaos for your own sanity. Little indulgences like spending five more minutes in the shower, soaking in the bath, reading a book, listening to a few tunes—these are all great calls to make. Hobbies are your little room of peace where you can go to find yourself again.

One of the best and most rewarding things for me is to journal. I enjoy doodling, sketching, and writing things down. You may not consider yourself much of a wordsmith, but trust me—just the action of writing something down, anything, can be so mentally freeing. It's also a great way of recording memories that you can one day go back and visit (like after you've made it through your first year of fatherhood!). There are even apps for those of us who are digitally attached.

And if you're really stuck, try the 1-3-5 method:

- Write down 1 thing you believe limits you from being a great dad.

- Write down 3 things you are grateful for as a dad.

- Write down 5 things that encourage and support you as a father.

Social

Sometimes, you need to just get out of crazy town. Going out and blowing off some steam by just feeling normal again is a great idea. On this subject, a former Navy SEAL had this to say:

> Men like me struggle with that. They hamster into their home lives or burrow into work, and claim a level of sacrifice that borders on martyrdom. Being home is valuable and important when it comes to raising children. However, it's not the mission objective. The truth is that parents need to be whole and complete if they are to teach their kids to be the same. If that means a few hours of poker on a Friday, or a couple of days in the mountains with the guys from time to time, then so be it (Davis, 2016, para. 16–17).

Now, don't use this as an excuse to go and play endless hours of golf every weekend or lock yourself in your mancave with the PlayStation, leaving your wife home alone to look after the baby. These are just meant to be small breaks every so often to give yourself a breather.

I was lucky enough in that Renee saw the benefit of me taking time out and agreed to me going camping for a weekend with one of my good friends. She saw it as an investment in my health, knowing I would come back recharged and fired up to keep going as a dad. And I knew that if she could do that for me, then I could allow her some time to also refresh. Parenting's a two-way street, after all!

- **Cheat Code:** Tactical breathing.

> Navy SEALS use this technique to calm their nerves when they're in hairy situations, and it works for dads, too. Breathe in, counting 1, 2, 3, 4. Stop and hold your breath as you count 1, 2, 3, 4 again. Exhale, counting 1, 2, 3, 4 one final time. You can do this three to five times if you like, and you'll be as sharp as a sniper!

I Get By With a Little Help

The Navy SEALS don't work alone. They're not mercenaries or lone wolves, but *teammates*. That's the core of their success: leaning on everyone's strengths so they can move forward together. If you want to survive your first year (and many more after that), you'll need a team around you. Besides you and your partner, this may be grandparents, friends, trusted babysitters, church groups, or other individuals you can trust.

There's an old proverb you've probably heard before—"It takes a village to raise a child" (Hinds, 2020). And while you may gawk at the prospect of handing over your precious treasure for a few moments or a whole night, there needs to come a time when you can, otherwise, you'll burn out and fail. Later, you're going to have to leave your kid in the care of a teacher, and much later, you're going to have to walk your daughter down the aisle and entrust her to her husband.

Ultimately, this is about more than giving yourself and your partner a break or having a date night away from the baby. It's about preparing your kid for *society*. She needs to be exposed to different kinds of people, learn to respond to others, and interact with those around her. Our kids have the right to experience a sense of belonging and community, and by reaching outside of the nucleus of our modern-day small families, we can give them exactly that. Life is about connections—just think of your own life and all the contacts you have, near and far. As Hodding Carter says, "There are two things we should give our children: one is roots and the other is wings" (Hinds, 2020).

So, how do you build a team that can help you and your daughter take on the world and survive? How do you expand your village? Well, the answer is to simply reach out and stay connected. You will start meeting other new parents, and you can invite them to events like birthday parties. Your neighbors, too, may become part of your lives more than you realize. Most people are just waiting for an invitation to be a part of your community!

I know for me, this was not an easy transition. My mom overstepped her boundaries many times, even to the point where I had to step in before Renee and her came to blows. I kid you not! The relationship soured a bit, and our village seemed to shrink. But I also had to learn an important lesson: that people are people. They make mistakes as much as we do, and if I struck others off the list because of things they said, did, or believed, I would end up with no one to reach out to. Truly, forgiveness, trust, and grace are sometimes necessary when it comes to family.

- **Cheat Code:** Say no.

    There are moments when it's better to decline people's requests and offers. You'll be inundated with visitors and do-gooders, so it's good to know when to draw the line and close the door politely.

Insider Info

Before I get ahead of myself and come across as the expert I said I wasn't, let me just remind you that I don't know everything. I figured out a lot of it as I went, and I'm still figuring out a lot of it as I go! And you know what? My journey, my village, and my mistakes are not yours. So, let me fling the net wide and catch a few other views and tips from dads who have been there and survived. Enjoy these insights:

- Saatvik has this to say:

    Look for the fun. Example: I was changing my daughter's diaper around six weeks. I lifted up her legs to wipe and suddenly she had a bowel movement that shot out at me, onto my pants, the bed, and our carpet. I thought it was hilarious. I was impressed. It was her world record. It also involved lots of cleaning. But it was also a world record (Minsberg, 2024, para. 3).

- Dan comes in with a different angle:

  The best advice I offer new parents is something I learned while having a son who spent the first four weeks of life in the hospital: only one parent is allowed to panic at a time… If both parents are a mess, then it's hard to hold each other up… your time will come to lean on someone else (Minsberg, 2024, para. 4).

- Dean learned a trick from his dad, and it works:

  If you lower your voice instead of raising it, nine times out of 10 the kid will too. My dad never, ever yelled. Well, maybe once or twice—and it was like an extinction level event when he did. That's because he recently told me that his strategy during our tantrums was to keep his voice down, because we would do it too (Christensen, 2022, para. 6).

- Stephen welcomes a shared laugh at his misfortune:

  Here's a tip from personal experience: If you put your child up on your shoulders, and then you hear a rapid thud-thud-thud-thud, that's because there is an operational ceiling fan directly above you. He's fine (Minsberg, 2024, para. 9).

- Aaron shares a handy little acronym that helps assess your kid's needs:

  If your kid is having a rough time, it's because he or she is hungry, agitated, lonely, or tired: H.A.L.T. It's not a magic word, by any means, but it does help you clue in to what might be upsetting your child. They're all basic needs, and sometimes they go unintentionally unmet (Christensen, 2022, para. 4).

- I want to follow Jim's advice, but it's hard to watch accidents happen. He simply says, "The hardest part of fatherhood is standing back and watching your child make their own mistakes. It is also one of the most important" (Minsberg, 2024).

- Brendyn from Germany echoes many dads' surprise when they forget to do this: "Lock the bathroom door while you're on the toilet. It's the only sanctuary in the house" (Minsberg, 2024).

- Kyle, an avid gamer, suggests a few changes to help the transition:

  When your exhausted wife brings you a screaming baby and you're in the middle of a Warzone match with "the boys," it's not going to be a pleasant experience for either you or your teammates. I've migrated to playing a lot more single player, campaign games that are infinitely pausable, and you can't lose your progress or get killed for being "AFK." Be prepared to drop the controller at a moment's notice, as that's what it takes to be a Gamer Dad (Jensen, 2024, para. 40).

- And lastly, I give you Mike's brilliant but cringeworthy pun: "Smile and Laugh… as much as you can. A joke is not a Dad joke until it becomes apparent" (Minsberg, 2024).

- **Cheat Code:** Vulgar Vs.

  Get used to words like vagina and vulva. Yip, it's not a man's world anymore… Using vague, silly euphemisms will catch you out later and cause confusion. So, take the plunge and use correct terms, and become used to talking openly about your daughter's body, then she will be comfortable talking to you about what she's going through.

The First-Year Rhythm Kit

Getting to Year One is not just a milestone for the baby but for Mom and Dad as well. At this stage, you'll take any win you can get!

On that note, check out the free cheat sheet I've made so you can keep a record of all the wins while feeling a little proud of what you've accomplished. Scan below and start celebrating.

Chapter 9:

Choosing for Tomorrow

Being a daddy's girl is like having permanent armor for the rest of your life.
—Marinela Reka

According to sources, parents make about 35,000 decisions every single day (Sippl, 2020). Many of those are done without thinking, especially since they're too tired to consciously weigh the options. It becomes robotic, really. Fortunately, though, most of those are not life-altering, earth-shattering judgments. They're simple day-to-day choices. It's the really big ones that matter... the ones that can follow you (or your daughter) through the rest of your life.

Take these dads, for example. If only they had a little more creativity and common sense when it came time to name their little girls:

- One daughter was christened "Mailliw," which is William, backward.

- Another girl's name is Sierra, which sounds fine, until you find out she's named for her dad's 1996 GMC SIERRA 1500 RED PICKUP!

- Or take Dominque, whose father forgot the second I.

- And then there's Ithaca, named after a gun company—not the Greek island!

   (Valko, 2024)

So, really, when it comes to the big decisions, it's not like picking out a shirt for the day or figuring out what to make for lunch. There are certain choices that have huge ripple effects, and it's best to weigh up everything before signing on the dotted line. In the end, all these major

79

crossroads events will determine your daughter's future and the legacy you want to pass on to her.

Family First

1,750. That's how many tough decisions parents have to make in the first year—about 34 every week (Aggarwal, 2020). These range from choosing names, deciding to breastfeed or use formula, and opting for disposable or cloth diapers, to which paediatrician to go to. The problem is that when you're required to make many of these choices, your sleep battery is bleeping, and you have a thousand voices all telling you to go in different directions. It's like being drugged on a game show and having to decide between door one or two with an audience screaming at you. You don't want to end up with the losing prize, but it's really hard to know if you should trust your gut or listen to the many experts!

In the end, most dads end up like Homer Simpson, the guy who just bumbles along, getting it mostly wrong! According to a survey (Aggarwal, 2020), these are the top 10 most difficult decisions that parents have to tackle during the 12 months after birth:

1. The baby's name
2. Breastfeeding versus formula
3. Childcare
4. Which formula to use
5. Where the baby sleeps
6. How to decorate the nursery
7. Which way to sleep train
8. Posting or not posting baby pics online

9. Finding the right doctor

10. Following what their own parents did

Here are a few others that didn't make it into this list but are worth mentioning since you'll come up against them sometime in your journey:

- Taking paternity leave
- When to start school (if ever)
- Sugar or no sugar
- How much screen time, if any
- When and how to discipline

We chose formula purely because breastfeeding (as rewarding and wonderful as it is) was a massive strain on Renee and the baby. It turned out to be exactly what fit for us as a family. Renee was less stressed, the baby was happier, and I even got to feed her during the nights. Our choice did not sit well with everyone, though. A few family members and friends made it clear that we were missing out, denying our daughter the best, and choosing a shortcut. And that was our first lesson in making decisions: *We will not please everyone.* This is for *us*, not them!

It was the same for most of the other 1,749 decisions we were faced with in our first year as parents. We knew there would be a fallout with certain people, but as long as we were both in agreement, then what did it matter? In the end, if something goes wrong, all the fingers will point at us, the mom and dad. Everyone else will join the game show audience and shake their heads. So, we needed to be sure that it was the best fit for us, and we were prepared to walk through whatever was on the other side of the door.

Another major talking point in the broader family was starting our daughter at daycare when she was six months old. There were a few shocked gasps, questions, and the expected "*Are you sure?*" It might be early for some, but we had done the research, had the chats, and after watching our little girl develop, it really felt like the right time. I noticed her confidence improve as she socialized with other babies and even toddlers. Apparently, this helps reduce any attachment anxiety that crops up around the 8–12-month mark, and it gave us a little bit of a break.

Now, not all of our decisions were good. We chose one direction, only to realize that we had to find an alternative that worked better for our situation. That meant swallowing our pride a bit as we backtracked down the hall of shame, hearing the predictable "*I told you so...*" echoes along the way. But you know what? That's just part of owning your choices. You are responsible for your kid, so you are answerable for the choices you make for them—no one else!

- **Cheat Code:** Don't fix everything.

    It's natural to want to solve problems and put things right. But your daughter doesn't always need that. She needs you to believe in her and her ability to figure things out for herself. That's giving her room to grow and showing you trust her.

A Moral Guide

Vanilla or chocolate? Chicken or beef? Marvel or DC?

Sometimes, picking one over the other is hard. I'm not a cut-and-dry decision maker, especially when it comes to mammoth, larger-than-life variables. And in the heat of the moment, when the pressure's on, I tend to make decisions based on my emotions. I'd rather just give in to my daughter to have a win-win situation (she gets her "thing" and there's peace again). But that's a short-term solution—not one that can sustain good parenting.

You can't toss a coin or roll the dice for these kinds of decisions. This is not an ice cream I'm ordering, or a movie I'm choosing—*it's a little life I'm handling.*

Having confidence in planning as a parent comes from having a personal moral compass. Truly, this helps to steer you clear of making rash, impulsive choices, and in their place, you get to make ones that are based on your life goals and principles. Instead of north, south, east, and west, there are just three cardinal points: passions, values, and beliefs (PVBs). In your relationship with your partner, if you can work these out and agree on them for your family, they will anchor you in storms and help you to steer toward clearer waters. But okay, what exactly are PVBs? Let's break them down.

Passions

A passion is a strong, enthusiastic desire for something. This is what inspires you to get out of bed and keep going. It could be hobbies, learning, helping people, being social, or even cars! You can have more than one passion, and even different ones from your wife. And that's a good thing!

So, why not list the things you're really fired up about? Your partner can do the same.

Values

These are the things you believe are important in how you live your life. They prioritize how you'll spend your time. There are too many to list here, ranging from security to loyalty to ingenuity or even beauty!

Write down your top few values and let your partner do the same.

It's interesting to see how your passions and values start working together. For example, say you're deeply passionate about football and really value spending quality time together as a family. Well, you might begin taking your crew out to watch a game on the weekends! Or, say, you have a passion for helping others who are not so well-off. In that case, you could help out at a local charity or soup kitchen!

Beliefs

These are the judgments about yourself and the world you live in. These come from your upbringing, who you hang out with, and your faith/religion. In short, whatever you believe in, you'll be committed to it. For a person who believes food that comes from animal byproducts is not right, they'll likely dedicate themselves to a vegan lifestyle. Or, if you believe in treating others equally, then you'll probably support racial equality and stick up for others.

Make a list of some of your beliefs. You might not get them all down or express them clearly, but start somewhere, as they'll become clearer as you go along. And again, have your partner jot down hers as well.

Now that you have an idea of where your own moral compass is pointing, it will make it easier to plan for your kid and their life. Without any doubt, your PVBs will determine how you raise your kid.

Strengths and Weaknesses

Now, it's time to look at your family's superpowers—and their kryptonite.

Don't reinvent things or change what's working. Instead, try to figure out what's good and stick with those things that align with your PVBs. If you're not sure, here are some easy questions to help you figure out your strengths:

- What do you like about your family?
- When are you happy with your clan?
- How is your unit unique?
- What do people compliment about your brood?

Now, identify the not-so-good things that require some work and attention. Ask these questions to get a better idea of them:

- When do you feel frustrated with your family?

- What makes you unhappy when you spend time with them?

- What do you want to change?

Every family has cracks—areas they know they lack in, and places they wish they could improve. Those who continue out of sync and ignore their weaknesses are the ones who practice reactive parenting—making choices according to emotions and circumstances.

However, by recognizing these flaws, you can begin working on bringing them into line with your PVBs. Parents who live intentionally, according to their compass points, are usually happier, more confident, and satisfied with the way they are living. It means recognizing that the time you spend with your kids is precious and limited, and that there's a long-lasting impact on how you decide to use that time (Huerta, 2018).

- **Cheat Code:** In charge, not in control.

Yes, there's a difference. Things can go wrong quickly, sending everything out the window. If you try to stay in control, you'll be a wreck. Staying in charge means recognizing that there are days when it just doesn't work, but you can pick yourself up, not let it get you down, and continue in the direction you intended.

Difficult Dilemmas

Wouldn't it be great if you had a magic crystal ball that could show you the outcome of your choices before you make them? That way, you'd avoid a few nasty falls, dodge the muddy parts, and sail through without a hitch, right? Well, the truth is, as great as your compass is, it'll never be this crystal ball. You're bound to get a little lost at times or find yourself in a jungle wondering which path is best. It's not going to be easy, but with the right intention, direction, and purpose, you can always have a goal of where you want to get your family.

No Clear-Cut Choice

It's not always going to be selecting good over bad. Some decisions are going to be choosing between two good options. Both schools look great, but which one is right *for you*? You sift through all the pros and cons only to come out with a stalemate at the end. Rational decision-making won't help because, well, both are equally good. I know for me, as a procrastinator, this type of conundrum makes me take a step back and do nothing. I want a black-and-white answer, a light from the sky, not this gray area of good versus good. But doing nothing is worse, and it will mean you and your family end up treading water.

So, you have to pick. Making a decision is more important than making the perfect one. You need to simply choose one and go with it. Scary, I know, but life has lots of those types of moments where forward motion is necessary.

Facing the Backlash

Jordan decided to save a bit of money by cutting his daughter's hair himself. What should have been a clever move, however, turned out to be an embarrassing hairstyle that landed him in the doghouse. After he lopped off more than two inches of golden locks, his partner's only comment on the incident is as follows: "It's 100 percent safe to say her dad is banned from cutting her hair again. It looked awful. It was a really big mess" (Norris, 2021). It's safe to say that some decisions don't win you popularity contests.

One of my best friends had his tubes tied the moment he got married! He and his wife just didn't want kids, ever. They intended to be free, to travel, and to live for themselves. And you know what? They're entitled to their decisions. But it sometimes causes tension, especially since he won't come near our little baby. Seriously, he has no interest in her. Even worse, his wife constantly reminds us how much free time she has because it's just the two of them. We've had to choose to limit time with them and find friends who we can identify with a bit more. And I gotta say, it's been tough on me!

Another couple shifted their lifestyle to accommodate their decision to be at home more. They took jobs that paid less just so they could spend more time with the kids (Williams, 2024). Sometimes, it means drawing lines, having boundaries, and sticking to their guns!

Leaving a Legacy

Your kid is growing up, and soon enough will even tell you what she aspires to be one day. Even she knows that there's a future that must be taken hold of. Whether she wants to be a unicorn doctor, a tree helper, a "please" officer, or a princess, you're going to need to be ready to help her realize her dreams. You might not be able to get her that unicorn doc degree, but you're still paving the way for her to grow into a kid, then a teen, and then an adult.

In your first year as a dad, or even back when your partner is still pregnant, you can begin laying down a blueprint for the life and legacy you want to leave for your daughter. This kind of forward-thinking is not just proactive and filled with purpose, but it will also allow you the space to enjoy your time together because you know exactly where you're both headed.

It may sound morbid, but start at the end. Picture this: You're all snug in your coffin surrounded by hundreds of people you know, all weeping, paying their respects. And then your daughter gets up to the podium… what is her eulogy? What are the words she says about her father? Regret, honor, anger, sorrow, love… or even nothing?

The point is, envisioning the end of the journey can help you prepare for it. It can make you more aware of how your life—the choices and the changes you need to make in it—molds you into the kind of father you hope she'll remember. Ask yourself these questions:

- When I am no longer here and my daughter is reflecting and remembering me, what do I want her most powerful memories of the time we had together to be?

- How do I want my obituary to read?

- What stories, memories, and influences do I want to leave behind for my daughter's kids and anyone else I influenced?

I don't know about you, but I hope I can be the kind of dad who leaves great memories for my daughter to hold onto.

How about Megi Garcia's recollection:

> I was the chubbiest among my three siblings and I had to sit on my dad's lap because I was too heavy for my mom. I fondly remember embracing him and falling asleep during the ride. Even when I woke up, I would pretend to be asleep so he would carry me until we reached the cinema (Valenzuela & Pastor, 2019, para. 1).

Or Tobi's midnight feasts with Dad:

> On random nights, he would whip up something in the kitchen, usually a big bowl of steak rice, chorizo rice, or a fun, interesting pasta. He brings the food up to the bedroom, wakes us all up, and within minutes we wipe the bowl clean. It wasn't the healthiest practice, but definitely made for a happy family, as well as tummy! (Valenzuela & Pastor, 2019, para. 14).

Ask yourself if your parenting style matches up with that of your partner. Do you see you two leaving the legacy you want for your little girl?

- **Emotional:** The way you speak, act, and rebuke all contribute to the type of emotional stamp you have on our kids. If you have a temper or are silent and absent, then that's what you're passing on. Just as you inherited things from your own parents, your kids will follow in your footsteps. Choosing to be more engaged, more loving, giving your daughter compliments, and building her up are ways you can rewrite the story you want to be read in her life.

- **Social:** This is all about the people you hang out with and the way you engage with your community. Your kids watch all of this. Instead of characters who only confuse and provoke, surround yourself with wholesome, mature, and solid friends and family. They will rub off on your kid as well. Getting involved, giving out, and being a part of something bigger than yourself is another way of extending your kid's horizons, building relationships, and letting her see beyond her own little world.

- **Spiritual:** Faith. In this world where there is so little that is constant, having something greater to hold onto and believe in is a game-changer. Your kid is a holistic being, not just a mouth to feed or a brain to educate, but a heart and soul that needs guidance and assurance. Meditating or praying with them can set the stage. Taking your daughter to church or on a retreat is a way of building her own belief system, one that will hold her in good stead through tough times.

When Karen found out she had a terminal disease, it changed her outlook on the time that she had left with her kids. She said, "Leaving a legacy doesn't have to always be serious or profound, it only has to be meaningful and authentic. Find a way to show love to your loved ones today" (Howell, 2021).

It's not all the big, flashy gifts or the expensive holidays that leave lasting imprints. It's the small things. Really, it's the boring, everyday things that are the ones that will be remembered more than all the others. Those bike rides, bedtime prayers, bubble baths, cookie bakes, silly song sessions, fort builds in the living room on rainy days, and ice creams on the beach. In the end, it's the time you spend with her that counts the most!

The Long-Term Girl Dad Kit

Where to go from here? Well, the hamster wheel doesn't stop for parents, and unless you have some sort of plan, you're going to just end up running in circles. Use this free printable to point your compass toward the future. Scan below to create a wonderful legacy for your daughter.

Conclusion

Robert Rogers was married for 12 years and was a father of four. That is, until a freak flash flood swept the family's minivan away, and Robert was the sole survivor. The kind of grief that comes with such a tragedy is enough to sink a man. But not Robert. In fact, he told reporters that he had a "life of no regrets" (Rogers, 2007). I'm sure he grieved and wept, like any person who had lost everything he held dear, but he also carried many treasures that kept him going through the dark times. See, he had a life full of wonderful memories—no guilt, no disappointments, no apologies.

Too many men are riddled with remorse because they *missed it* as a father. They feel as though they could have and should have done more. *If only...*

Dr. Bruce Robinson, a lung physician from Australia, became deeply concerned after speaking to his male patients. They were all getting to the end of their lives, with little time left. What shocked the doctor was the deep and profound regret so many of them felt over their relationship with their daughters (Myler, 2022).

Look, having a kid is not a right. It's not a guaranteed part of life. Certainly not something you do *just because you can*. Having a kid is also not a burden, or even... a responsibility. Too many men have this approach to their role as a father, and so they miss it completely. They're good providers, but there's simply no relationship. And at the end of their lives, all they have is a sense of loss, because they just don't actually know their daughters, and their little girls don't know them either.

Being a father is a *privilege*!

Roger Roberts realized this, which is why he could proudly say that he had no regrets! His secret was making the most of moments. Not every moment, mind you—that's impossible to do (and you'll break yourself trying to always be the coolest, funniest, bravest, most sensitive dad). But between all the chaos, there are gaps where you can choose, deliberately and intentionally, to create a beautiful memory. It doesn't take a planned outing or a list of great things to do. It's simply about generously sharing your time with your daughter.

When Robert's seven-year-old daughter asked him if they could finish the birdhouse he had promised to complete, he had a list of legitimate excuses. But instead, he had told her, "Let's make a memory" (Roberts, 2007). That was seven weeks before the accident.

I don't want to be a sorry excuse for a father. I know I'll mess it up and fall short many times, but I want to try to be the best that my little girl has. And since you've read this far into the book, I take it you do too! So, let's make the most of those fleeting moments.

- Don't be in such a rush.

- Don't be so dismissive.

- Don't be so distracted.

- Don't put off doing things together.

- Don't be off in your head somewhere else.

When a moment comes along (usually out of the blue, like a shooting star), be there for as long as it takes. Fully, consciously, wholeheartedly. Those are the small treasures that you will carry with you. Those are the memories your daughter will keep close to her heart as she grows up, gets married, and moves away.

In Robert's words, "Today, start living a life of no regrets with your family. Make a memory. None of us is guaranteed tomorrow" (Rogers, 2007).

Now, allow me to squeeze in one last cheat code here. This one is my favorite because it lends itself to the kind of impulsive idiot I am sometimes. But I find that it pays dividends in huge amounts, sometimes creating the best life memories I have.

- **Cheat Code:** For no reason.

    Grab an ice cream cone, play a board game, stay in bed together. You don't have to have a reason for it... That's why it's so beautiful. Your daughter will love it, and so will you. Living life is more than changing diapers, paying bills, and ticking off boxes. It's about seizing the moments that aren't even there.

And so... what are you waiting for? Put this book down. You should be out there with your amazing family, making the most of what you have! Be the great dad you already are.

The Remember-and-Laugh Kit

Before you go, here's a bonus cheat sheet just for fun so you can look back one day with a laugh and a tear as you reflect on these crazy early years of having a daughter! Scan below and enjoy!

Everything you've just read? That's how it happened — from where I stood.

But my wife Renee? She remembers it differently. Behind every new dad is a new mom finding her way too. While I was fumbling through bottles and self-doubt, my wife Renee was quietly carrying the weight of a thousand invisible things. Soon, she shares her story – her way. The next one's for the moms.

As I've shared my journey of becoming a girl dad with you, I hope you'll share yours with me in exchange. Really, how has this book impacted or helped you unleash your super girl dad energy? I'd be honored if you let me know by leaving a review of the book on Amazon. Your feedback means more than you know, and it helps other new dads find the support they need too. Just scan the QR code below to leave a review. Thanks!

To explore the full *Girl Dad Energy* series, including the guided journal and future books — scan to visit:

Thank you for reading, for showing up, and for being the kind of dad who cares.

– Tyler

References

Aggarwal, N. (2020, July 9). *Parents make 1,750 tough decisions in baby's first year, survey says.* Thebump.com; The Bump. https://www.thebump.com/news/tough-parenting-decisions-first-year-baby-life

Alzahrani, A. (2023, December 2). *It's OK to make mistakes. especially as parents.* The Good Men Project. https://goodmenproject.com/featured-content/its-ok-to-make-mistakes-especially-as-parents/

Axani, J. (2025). *Why being a new dad is harder than we admit.* Shiftcollab.com; Shift Collab. https://www.shiftcollab.com/blog/why-being-a-new-dad-is-harder-than-we-admit

Beck, A. (n.d.). Quote. In Khurana, S. (2019). *13 quotes and words to praise a baby girl.* ThoughtCo. https://www.thoughtco.com/baby-girl-quotes-2832753

Brey, J. (2023, August 7). Linkedin.com. https://www.linkedin.com/posts/justinbrey_forgiveness-mistakesarelessons-mondaymindset-activity-7094317293349851136-_ccR/?trk=public_profile_like_view

Brown, J. (2021, March 25). *What I learned about marriage the first year of being a parent.* Fatherly. https://www.fatherly.com/love-money/what-we-learned-about-marriage-the-first-of-parenting

Brill, A. (n.d.). Quote. In Soderlund, A. (2022, August 31). *50 inspiring quotes for those really hard parenting moments.* Nurture and Thrive. https://nurtureandthriveblog.com/parenting-quotes-hard-moments/

Bustamante, C. S. (2022, June 16). *Tactical diaper bags and other fathers' day tips from a marine officer.* Military Health System. https://health.mil/News/Articles/2022/06/16/Tactical-Diaper-Bags-and-Other-Fathers-Day-Tips-from-a-Marine-Officer?type=Articles&page=7

Cassidy, A. (2023, January 27). *The startling difference between raising boys and raising girls.* IMAGE.ie. https://www.image.ie/self/the-startling-difference-between-raising-boys-and-raising-girls-155515

Child, L. (2012). *Jack Reacher's rules.* Delacorte Press.

Chow, E. K. (2016, June 16). *The difference between a dad and a father.* Medium. https://robinhoodnyc.medium.com/the-difference-between-a-dad-and-a-father-e00712c6e055

Christensen, M. (2022, September 26). *44 pieces of life-changing parenting advice, from dads who've been there.* Fatherly. https://www.fatherly.com/life/life-changing-parenting-advice-dads

Cosslett, R. L. (2022, August 22). The struggle of fatherhood is real - so why are new dads often invisible in NHS advice? *The Guardian.* https://www.theguardian.com/commentisfree/2022/aug/22/no-one-tells-you-how-hard-dad-new-parent-pregnancy-birth

Cummings, E. (2017, January 12). *11 dads describe the first time they saw their newborn child.* The Herald-Times. https://www.heraldtimesonline.com/story/lifestyle/2017/01/12/11-dads-describe-the-first-time-they-saw-their-newborn-child/46788865/

Davis, E. (2016, June 17). *How I used my military skills to become a better father.* TIME; nextgen. https://time.com/4373161/navy-seal-fatherhood/

Dent, M. (2016, May 26). *The power of the parental pause.* Maggie Dent. https://www.maggiedent.com/blog/power-parental-pause/

Dubinsky, D. (2023). *Laugh and learn: New parents share their most embarrassing mistakes.* BabyCenter. https://www.babycenter.com/baby/newborn-baby/laugh-and-learn-new-parents-share-their-most-embarrassing-mi_9792

Dude Dad. (2017, June 16). *Fathers describe birth.* YouTube. https://www.youtube.com/watch?v=50Be0IzIlZA

Duhamel, J. (n.d.). Quote. In Hershberger, D. (2022, February 25). *The best sleeping baby quotes.* Fun with Mama. https://www.funwithmama.com/sleeping-baby-quotes/

Ea, P. (2025). *Millennial dads spend 3 times as much time with their kids than previous generations - study finds - prince EA | filmmaker, speaker, creator.* Prince EA | Filmmaker, Speaker, Creator. https://www.princeea.com/millennial-dads-spend-3-times-as-much-time-with-their-kids-than-previous-generations-study-finds/

Ephron, N. (n.d.). Quote. In Gillett, T. (2016, June 17). *How do you keep your marriage strong after having kids?* Raised Good. https://raisedgood.com/keep-marriage-strong-kids/

Fernandez, C. (2019, March 26). *These Father's Day quotes describe the precious bond between a dad and his child.* Oprah Daily. https://www.oprahdaily.com/life/relationships-love/g26900517/fathers-day-quotes/

Gannon, A. (2023, December 3). *Relationship advice for new parents in first year of parenthood.* Expectful. https://expectful.com/articles/first-year-parenthood-relationship

Gard, J. (2024, December 30). *From bellies to babies antenatal & postnatal classes*. From Bellies to Babies Antenatal & Postnatal Classes. https://belliestobabies.co.nz/resources-sharing-my-knowledge/celebrating-fatherhood-rituals-and-traditions-for-new-dads

Gordon, S. (2023, November 16). *15 things dads should know when raising baby girls*. Parents. https://www.parents.com/baby/new-parent/fatherhood/dads-and-daughters/

Heger, E. (n.d.). *When to start reading to your baby*. BabyCenter. https://www.babycenter.com/baby/baby-development/reading-to-your-baby_368

Herenda, D. (2022, June 20). *18 celebs who are dedicated stepparents*. BuzzFeed. https://www.buzzfeed.com/devinherenda/celebs-who-stepped-up-as-stepparents

Hermans, J. (2023, July 11). *Intentional parenting: A method that works for all*. Jenna Hermans - Chaos to Calm. https://jennahermans.com/chaos-to-calm-blog/intentional-parenting/

Hinds, S. (2020, July 22). *"It takes a village to raise a child" — African proverb. Here's why it's true*. Medium. https://medium.com/@sherlaine.hinds/it-takes-a-village-to-raise-a-child-african-proverb-heres-why-it-s-true-53122b998801

Homme, J. H. (2022, May 10). *The first parent freakout: Baby falls*. Mayo Clinic Press. https://mcpress.mayoclinic.org/parenting/the-first-parent-freakout-baby-falls/

Howell, A. (2021, May 6). *21 ways to start building your legacy today*. Inheritance of Hope. https://inheritanceofhope.org/21-ways-to-start-building-your-legacy-today

Huerta, D. (2018, September 28). *Why your kids need intentional parents.* Focus on the Family. https://www.focusonthefamily.com/parenting/why-your-kids-need-intentional-parents/

Hund, J. (n.d.). Quote. In Hallmark staff. (2021, April). *85+ heartfelt and meaningful Father's Day quotes.* Hallmark Ideas & Inspiration. https://ideas.hallmark.com/articles/fathers-day-ideas/fathers-day-quotes/

Iftikhar, N. (2020, December 21). *Baby bath temperature: What's the ideal? Plus, more bathing tips.* Healthline. https://www.healthline.com/health/baby/baby-bath-temperature

Jensen, K. (2024, March 12). *New dad survival guide: Gamer edition.* Medium. https://medium.com/@ultimatedad87/new-dad-survival-guide-gamer-edition-f083dc4bb3ae

Kinsey, T. C. (2016, August 30). *Why every parent should suffer a total wipe out.* TIME; Time. https://time.com/4473133/parenting-advice-mistakes/

LoRe, A. (2025, January 28). *Do newborn babies need a sleep schedule?* Huckleberry. https://huckleberrycare.com/blog/foundational-newborn-sleep-habits

Madrigal, A. C. (2013, December 24). *Why men fear small babies.* The Atlantic. https://www.theatlantic.com/business/archive/2013/12/why-men-fear-small-babies/282616/

Marek Demcak. (2022, December 10). *How to manage priorities when you become a parent.* Linkedin.com. https://www.linkedin.com/pulse/how-manage-priorities-when-you-become-parent-marek-demcak/

Miller, K. (2017, November 9). *This woman used a balloon to demonstrate what giving birth is like and parents-to-be are obsessed.* SELF. https://www.self.com/story/this-woman-used-a-balloon-to-demonstrate-what-giving-birth-is-like

Minsberg, T. (2024, June 14). *The best advice for dads (according to dads).* The New York Times. https://www.nytimes.com/interactive/2024/06/14/well/family/dad-advice-life-fathers.html

Molitor, B. D., & Molitor, K. (2007). *Girl's passage father's duty.* Emerald Books.

Myler, C. (2022, August 30). *Dads and daughters in the 21st century.* Maggie Dent. https://www.maggiedent.com/blog/dads-and-daughters-in-the-21st-century/

Nadeau, A. (2019, September 13). *75 hilarious quotes about dads and being a father.* The Dad. https://www.thedad.com/75-hilarious-quotes-about-dads-and-being-a-father/

Norris, S. (2021, August 28). *Home haircut goes horrendously wrong.* News; news.com.au — Australia's leading news site. https://www.news.com.au/lifestyle/parenting/home-haircut-goes-horrendously-wrong-as-dad-goes-rogue-on-daughter/news-story/65c292000a219d05ee626acc51c348fe

Patel, R. (2023, July 17). *"I've missed more than 9000 shots in my career..."* Impact Network. https://www.impactnetwork.org/latest-news/ive-missed-more-than-9000-shots-in-my-career

Peerspective. (2024, October 24). *Being a dad in a "perfect" world: Why making mistakes is okay.* Medium; Pragmatic Wisdom. https://medium.com/a-little-stoic-wisdom/being-a-dad-in-a-perfect-world-why-making-mistakes-is-okay-10bc2062e816

Pittman, F. (n.d.). Quote. In Jolade. (2020, June 21). *The imperfection of fatherhood.* Akin Akingbogun. https://akinakingbogun.com/2020/06/21/lessons-from-imperfect-fathers/

Pittman, F. (n.d.). Quote. In Saye, K. (2023, March 19). *70+ wonderful, inspiring Father's Day quotes for cards from son, daughter for a husband, new dads, UK.* Cardology. https://cardology.co.uk/blogs/news/inspirational-fathers-day-quotes-for-cards

Porter, D. (2023, September 21). *10 benefits of a strong father-daughter relationship.* Marriage Advice - Expert Marriage Tips & Advice. https://www.marriage.com/advice/parenting/father-daughter-relationship/

Rae, E. (2022, January 22). *Dads mental health & the pressures on the modern dad - an interview with Elliott Rae.* The Nourish App. https://www.thenourishapp.com/post/dads-mental-health-the-pressures-on-the-modern-dad

Reilly, K. C. (2021, June 20). *The power of a girl dad.* Newsweek. https://www.newsweek.com/power-girl-dad-opinion-1596063

Redmond-Fisher, K. (2022, October 18). *Mental health and wellbeing tips for new dads.* Www.bupa.co.uk. https://www.bupa.co.uk/newsroom/ourviews/new-dad-mental-health-tips

Reka, M. (n.d.). Quote. In Parkerton, M. (2023, June 17). *100 sweet daddy-daughter quotes.* Parade: Entertainment, Recipes, Health, Life, Holidays. https://parade.com/1333841/michelle-parkerton/father-daughter-quotes/

Reynolds, R. (n.d.). Quote. In Parkerton, M. (2023, June 17). *100 sweet daddy-daughter quotes.* Parade: Entertainment, Recipes, Health,

Life, Holidays. https://parade.com/1333841/michelle-parkerton/father-daughter-quotes/

Rogers, R. (2025). *Parenting with no regrets before it's too late*. Focus on the Family Canada. https://www.focusonthefamily.ca/content/parenting-with-no-regrets-before-its-too-late

Sethi, A. (2025). *Boys will be boys, girls will be girls from birth*. Cnn.com. https://edition.cnn.com/2008/HEALTH/family/08/20/parenting.gender/index.html

Silva, G. D. (2024, December 3). *The vital role of dad-baby bonding: Activities and benefits for 0-3-month-olds - fathers 4 justice south africa*. Fathers 4 Justice South Africa. https://www.f4j.co.za/2024/12/03/dad-baby-bonding-activities-0-3-months/?v=eacb463a8002

Sippl, A. (2020, May 25). *Every parent's guide to decision fatigue (part 1)*. Life Skills Advocate. https://lifeskillsadvocate.com/blog/every-parents-guide-to-decision-fatigue/

Smith, I., & Macdonald, J. (2022, May 25). *Surprise! How men react when becoming a dad isn't part of the plan*. The Conversation. https://theconversation.com/surprise-how-men-react-when-becoming-a-dad-isnt-part-of-the-plan-182141

Stewart, D. H. (2023). *Sex and the new dad*. BabyCenter. https://www.babycenter.com/family/fatherhood/sex-and-the-new-dad_3693

Stoop, D., & Stoop, J. (2005). *The complete marriage book*. Fleming H. Revell Company.

Taylor, I. (2024, October 24). *"The anxiety was debilitating. I didn't see it coming": Why new dads need more support*. Men's Health.

https://www.menshealth.com/uk/mental-strength/a62369602/why-new-fathers-need-more-support/

Thompson, R. (2022). *The powerful influence of a father: 4 things every kid needs from their dad.* Berean Baptist Church. https://www.bereanmn.com/family-ministry-blog/the-powerful-influence-of-a-father-4-things-every-kid-needs-from-their-dad/

Tommy's. (2022, June 15). *How does pregnancy affect fathers and partners.* Www.tommys.org. https://www.tommys.org/pregnancy-information/dads-and-partners/how-pregnancy-affects-you

Valko, A. (2024, January 5). *17 questionable names given by fathers.* BuzzFeed. https://www.buzzfeed.com/alanavalko/terrible-names-fathers-gave-their-kids

Valenzuela, N., & Pastor, P. (2019, June 16). *What is your favorite memory of your dad from your childhood?* https://lifestyle.inquirer.net/338216/what-is-your-favorite-memory-of-your-dad-from-your-childhood/

Vallerand, N. (2020, November). *Parenting is a team effort.* Naitreetgrandir.com. https://naitreetgrandir.com/en/feature/parenting-is-a-team-effort/

Watkins, A., Rankin, J., & McGovern, R. (2024, November 28). *Four struggles men face during the transition to fatherhood.* The Conversation. https://theconversation.com/four-struggles-men-face-during-the-transition-to-fatherhood-243771

Williams, A. (2024, December 25). *10 life decisions that surprise first-time parents.* Moonkie. https://moonkieshop.com/blogs/news/10-life-decisions-that-surprise-first-time-parents?srsltid=AfmBOoq3QFw-TlkjIc8GdrlWod1b5hwOcAApoSm8QcCT8V3lnMEyzbHo

Printed in Dunstable, United Kingdom